MAKING SENSE OF
MATHEMATICS
FOR TEACHING
the Small Group

JULI K. DIXON

LISA A. BROOKS

MELISSA R. CARLI

Solution Tree | Press

a division of
Solution Tree

555 North Morton Street
Bloomington, IN 47404
800.733.6786 (toll free) / 812.336.7700

FAX: 812.336.7790

email: info@SolutionTree.com
SolutionTree.com

Visit **go.SolutionTree.com/mathematics** to download the free reproducibles in this book.

Printed in the United States of America

Library of Congress Cataloging-in-Publication Data

Names: Dixon, Juli K., author. | Brooks, Lisa A., author. | Carli, Melissa
   R., author.
Title: Making sense of mathematics for teaching the small group / Juli K.
   Dixon, Lisa A. Brooks, and Melissa R. Carli.
Description: Bloomington, IN : Solution Tree Press, [2019] | Includes
   bibliographical references and index.
Identifiers: LCCN 2018000575 | ISBN 9781947604049 (perfect bound)
Subjects: LCSH: Mathematics--Study and teaching. | Group work in education.
Classification: LCC QA11 .D56287 2019 | DDC 372.7/044--dc23 LC record available at https://lccn.loc.gov/2018000575

Solution Tree
Jeffrey C. Jones, CEO
Edmund M. Ackerman, President

Solution Tree Press
President and Publisher: Douglas M. Rife
Editorial Director: Sarah Payne-Mills
Art Director: Rian Anderson
Managing Production Editor: Kendra Slayton
Production Editor: Alissa Voss
Senior Editor: Amy Rubenstein
Copy Editor: Jessi Finn
Proofreader: Miranda Addonizio
Text and Cover Designer: Abigail Bowen

Acknowledgments

My deepest love and gratitude to my very special small group who always supports my endeavors, wherever they might take us: my daughters, Alex and Jessica, and my husband, Marc.

—Juli Dixon

My amazing family is my inspiration. To my husband, John—thank you for your endless encouragement and for always believing in me. To my children, Anthony, Sarah, Wyatt, and Darby—you motivate me to dream big!

—Lisa Brooks

I'm so thankful for the two men in my life who supported me through this entire journey: my husband, Matthew, and my newly born son, Luke. Matthew, thank you for being my rock throughout not only this writing process but all of life's adventures.

—Melissa Carli

A special thanks to the students and teachers at Sabal Point Elementary School for sharing your mathematical thinking with us. Thank you, Christina Langdon, Maura Olvey, and the University of Central Florida for making it all possible. Thanks also to Alissa Voss for ensuring that our message is clear, and to Jeff Jones and Douglas Rife for investing in our vision. To our reviewers, thank you for taking the time to think deeply and provide such helpful feedback about our work. To our DNA Math family, thank you for all your support.

—Juli Dixon, Lisa Brooks, and Melissa Carli

Solution Tree Press would like to thank the following reviewers:

Jennifer Basner
Fifth-Grade Teacher
Berlin Community School
Berlin, New Jersey

Cheryl Cantin
Mathematics, Science, and
    Technology Consultant
Eastern Townships School Board
Magog, Quebec, Canada

Rebecca Elder
Sixth-Grade Teacher
McMillan Elementary School
Murray, Utah

Laura Hunovice
Elementary Mathematics Specialist
Carroll County, Maryland

Karen S. Karp
Visiting Professor, Mathematics Education
Johns Hopkins University
Baltimore, Maryland

Matthew Larson
President
National Council of Teachers of Mathematics
Lincoln, Nebraska

Sarah Reed
Hybrid and S.T.R.E.A.M. Teacher
Hazelwood Elementary School
Louisville, Kentucky

Donald Sarazen
Fifth-Grade Teacher
White Knoll Elementary School
West Columbia, South Carolina

Helen Spruill
Mathematics Coach
PS 503 The School of Discovery
Brooklyn, New York

Becky Walker
Director of Learning Services and
    Mathematics Specialist
Cooperative Educational Service Agency 7
    Mathematics/Science Center
Green Bay, Wisconsin

Gabriel Ward
K–8 Mathematics Teacher on Special Assignment
Hacienda La Puente Unified School District
City of Industry, California

Visit **go.SolutionTree.com/mathematics** to download the free reproducibles in this book.

Table of Contents

CHAPTER 3
Discourse in Small-Group Instruction **49**

EPILOGUE
How to Tie It All Together **67**

APPENDIX A
Sample Lesson Plan for Grades K–2 Using TQE Process Lesson-Planning Tool . . . **71**

APPENDIX B
Sample Lesson Plan for Grades 3–5 Using TQE Process Lesson-Planning Tool . . . **73**

About the Authors

Juli K. Dixon, PhD, is a professor of mathematics education at the University of Central Florida (UCF) in Orlando. She coordinates the award-winning Lockheed Martin/UCF Academy for Mathematics and Science for the K–8 master of education program as well as the mathematics track of the doctoral program in education. Prior to joining the faculty at UCF, Dr. Dixon was a secondary mathematics educator at the University of Nevada, Las Vegas, and a public school mathematics teacher in urban school settings at the elementary, middle, and secondary levels.

She is a prolific writer who has authored and coauthored books, textbooks, chapters, and articles. She is also a lead author on the *Making Sense of Mathematics for Teaching* professional development book and video series as well as for K–12 school mathematics textbooks with Houghton Mifflin Harcourt. Especially important to Dr. Dixon is the need to teach each and every student. She often shares her personal story of supporting her own children with special needs to learn mathematics in an inclusive setting. Dr. Dixon published *A Stroke of Luck: A Girl's Second Chance at Life* with her daughter, Jessica Dixon. A sought-after speaker, Dr. Dixon has delivered keynotes and other presentations throughout North America.

Dr. Dixon received a bachelor's degree in mathematics and education from the State University of New York at Potsdam, a master's degree in mathematics education from Syracuse University, and a doctorate in curriculum and instruction with an emphasis in mathematics education from the University of Florida. Dr. Dixon is a leader in Dixon Nolan Adams Mathematics.

To learn more about Dr. Dixon's work supporting children with special needs, visit www.astrokeofluck.net, or to learn more about Dr. Dixon's work supporting teachers, follow @thestrokeofluck on Twitter.

Lisa A. Brooks, EdD, is an associate lecturer at the University of Central Florida. She teaches classes in mathematics and science education in the elementary education program. She is an Inclusive Education Faculty Fellow and a Graduate Faculty Scholar. Her research is focused on helping teachers facilitate student discourse to increase conceptual understanding of mathematics. Dr. Brooks has been an educator since 1992. She has experience teaching elementary and middle school students.

Dr. Brooks is co-author of *Making Sense of Mathematics for Teaching Grades K–2.* She is also a published author of multiple articles in state, national, and international journals. She provides professional development throughout North America and has experience presenting at conferences for educators, school leaders, district leaders, and teacher educators.

Dr. Brooks received a bachelor's degree in elementary education from the University of Central Florida. She is a Lockheed Martin Scholar with a master's degree in K–8 mathematics and science education. She earned a doctorate in curriculum and instruction with a focus on mathematics education from the University of Central Florida. She is certified in elementary education, primary education, and English for Speakers of Other Languages (ESOL).

To learn more about Dr. Brooks's work, follow @DrBrooksla on Twitter.

Melissa R. Carli is a curriculum program specialist for Lake County Schools. In her role, Melissa supports schools and teachers by facilitating collaboration around the Common Core State Standards in order to assist in preparing for and implementing rigorous mathematics instruction. Her focus is on providing teachers with the tools and knowledge necessary to help their students think critically around mathematical content. Melissa has taught at the elementary and middle school levels and served as both a mathematics coach and department chair.

Melissa has presented her work at local, state, and national conferences as well as in school districts throughout North America, focusing on using effective instructional practices in mathematics. She is a member of the Florida Association of Mathematics Supervisors, Florida Council of Teachers of Mathematics, and National Council of Teachers of Mathematics (NCTM).

She earned a bachelor's degree and master's degree in education from the University of Florida. Melissa also earned a master's degree in educational leadership.

To learn more about Melissa Carli's work, follow @MCarliLovesMath on Twitter.

To book Juli K. Dixon, Lisa A. Brooks, or Melissa R. Carli for professional development, contact pd@ SolutionTree.com.

Introduction

Education is not the filling of a pail, but the lighting of a fire.

—W. B. Yeats

If you spend much time in a traditional elementary school classroom, you will likely see at least a portion of the mathematics block devoted to small-group instruction. Such time is often characterized by groups of students rotating through *centers* or *stations*, where students work on mathematics independently or in small groups. One group might start at the computer station, where students work on individualized learning programs; another group of students might play an educational game together; and students in a third group might work on their own to complete problems on a worksheet. Activities in these centers often vary; however, during small-group instruction, the existence of the *pulled small group*—the group of students that the teacher pulls to receive direct support—seems to be consistent.

Based on your own experience teaching or conducting classroom observations, you might picture a pulled small group as a teacher and students sitting together at a kidney-shaped table. The teacher sits in the center of the curve, and the students sit around the outside of the curve, each facing the teacher. It is typical for teachers to use this common pulled-small-group setup to offer support based on individualized student needs.

In our roles as mathematics teachers and educators, mathematics researchers, coaches, and teachers, we have observed a wide variety of lessons in which teachers engage students in small-group instruction. Working with school districts throughout North America, it has become obvious to us that this aspect of mathematics instruction—what we call *small-group instruction*, or engaging students in learning in a pulled-small-group setting—is in need of refinement. When observing small-group instruction, we typically see a teacher explaining how to solve a problem to a group of students using a particular procedure. The students are then offered the opportunity with a similar problem to replicate the teacher's steps on their own. When students struggle, the teacher attempts to scaffold student learning by explaining the procedure again using the numbers in the new problem. What is missing from this scenario are opportunities for students to think critically, take ownership of their learning, and make sense of the procedure. Without these opportunities, students are unable to transfer and apply their mathematics understanding to new situations. Small-group instruction can provide a venue for closely examining individual student thinking and facilitating students to make connections among mathematics concepts; however, the way it is typically being used does not allow teachers to truly get to know their students' existing understandings so that teachers can tailor their actions and responses to students' individual needs.

Our motivation for writing this book is to share effective small-group instruction practices and to unpack the purposes of and best practices for small-group instruction. Although small-group instruction

1

is deeply embedded in many elementary mathematics classrooms, both administrators and teachers often neglect examining the purpose and quality of instruction during small-group time. We encourage administrators to read this book alongside their teachers so they build a shared image of what effective elements lead to high-quality small-group instruction in mathematics. As you read about each element, we urge you to deeply reflect on how these elements occur in your classroom or the classrooms you support. How does your current instruction align with the encouraged practices throughout this book? How does your belief system and philosophy of small-group instruction promote or hinder the type of thinking required of students? As you read, allow the material to challenge your beliefs and current instructional practices.

In this introduction, we first describe the need for high-quality practices specifically tailored for small-group mathematics instruction. We then describe the purposes of small-group instruction. We anticipate that what you learn through this book will motivate you to dig deeper into ways you might support students to learn mathematics. For this reason, we also direct you to additional resources that may guide your instruction of elementary mathematics.

High-Quality Small-Group Mathematics Instruction

Many teachers use small-group interventions for mathematics in ways similar to small-group interventions during reading instruction. As a result, small-group work during mathematics instruction often mirrors that of reading. For example, one aspect of small-group instruction in reading that teachers often transfer to small-group instruction in mathematics is the use of *gradual release of responsibility*. In this instructional method, the teacher begins by modeling ("I do"), then the class practices as a whole group ("We do"), and finally the students practice independently ("You do"; Fisher & Frey, 2014). This strategy, which San Diego State University professors of educational leadership Douglas Fisher and Nancy Frey (2014) describe, has been used extensively during reading instruction; however, it can undermine best practices in small-group mathematics instruction. Mathematics instruction requires a different model to facilitate deep understanding. Lynn S. Fuchs, Douglas Fuchs, and Donald L. Compton (2012) provide a critical analysis of interventions for mathematics at the elementary level. Their research identifies strengths and limitations of using strategies based on correcting errors and procedural computations. While they state that strategies focusing on procedures are effective for some students within distinct topics of mathematics, they emphasize that not all students benefit from that type of intervention. They also note that students do not necessarily transfer knowledge to other mathematical topics. If the goal is to close the achievement gap and to build conceptual understanding of mathematics, different approaches must be explored.

Research compiled in *Principles to Actions: Ensuring Mathematical Success for All* (National Council of Teachers of Mathematics [NCTM], 2014) suggests that students are more likely to develop conceptual understanding of mathematical topics when they are provided opportunities to engage in productive discourse. Teachers can help ensure that students engage in productive discourse when they encourage them to share reasoning, build off one another's mathematical understanding, and make meaningful connections through the use of various tools. These connections are more likely to last and help students make associations within and across concepts (NCTM, 2014). Thus, rather than telling students about mathematics and showing them procedures to follow, the focus should be on *listening* to students and *facilitating* their connections to important mathematical concepts, especially during small-group instruction, where there are such excellent opportunities to gain access to students' thinking.

Throughout *Making Sense of Mathematics for Teaching the Small Group*, we provide detailed suggestions, aligned with the research shared in *Principles to Actions* (NCTM, 2014), for how teachers can improve the small-group model of mathematics instruction. We highlight how to facilitate understanding by using effective questioning and responding to student talk as students provide evidence of their learning, and we address how to engage students in meaningful tasks through the eight Standards for Mathematical Practice contained within the Common Core State Standards for mathematics (National Governors Association Center for Best Practices [NGA] & Council of Chief State School Officers [CCSSO], 2010). We will refer to the eight Mathematical Practices at various times throughout the book.

1. Make sense of problems and persevere in solving them.

2. Reason abstractly and quantitatively.

3. Construct viable arguments and critique the reasoning of others.

4. Model with mathematics.

5. Use appropriate tools strategically.

6. Attend to precision.

7. Look for and make use of structure.

8. Look for and express regularity in repeated reasoning.

It is important to consider how we engage students in these Mathematical Practices. They bring to the forefront the skills we look to develop as students build understanding of mathematical concepts. Throughout the book we discuss how the questions and tasks teachers choose support students to engage in the various Mathematical Practices and help them develop as proficient mathematical problem solvers.

As we begin to explore best practices in small groups, it will be helpful to first consider if, and when, the small-group structure is beneficial for a given learning goal.

Purposes of Small-Group Instruction

It is important to consider whether pulled-small-group instruction is appropriate for your particular learning goal. We encourage you to make this instructional decision consciously. The questions of when and how frequently to pull small groups during mathematics instruction is a key aspect of the decision-making process. Furthermore, the students' needs should determine the necessity of pulled-small-group instruction, rather than an expectation that you incorporate small groups into mathematics instruction each and every day. In addition to working with students on grade-appropriate tasks in settings where the teacher has greater access to the thinking of each and every student, there are two main reasons why the pulled small group is typically used: (1) intervention and (2) enrichment.

Intervention

Teachers commonly view small-group instruction as a time to provide intervention for students who are struggling with mathematical concepts. One form of intervention during work in the small group is to support students by providing instruction on prerequisite concepts and skills. For example, if several students are struggling with adding and subtracting fractions with unlike denominators because they have difficulty generating equivalent fractions, then it would help to pull this group of students and provide instruction on this skill. Most likely, the students are having difficulty generating equivalent fractions because they lack conceptual understanding of fraction equivalence. In this example, the purpose of providing intervention is clear but implementation is equally important. If the intervention consists of providing more of the same instruction to the struggling students, then an opportunity for learning is missed. On the other hand, an effective intervention might afford them the opportunity to use visual representations in a small group setting; through those visual representations, they can gain conceptual understanding of the prerequisite skill. In this particular case, the students could be given a task that requires them to find equivalent fractions using tools. These tools could take the form of drawings, paper cut-outs, or Cuisenaire Rods, to name a few. In a small-group setting, the teacher would also have the opportunity to diagnose each student's specific struggles and address them with tailored supports.

Enrichment

Although not used as frequently for this purpose, small-group instruction can also be an avenue for providing enrichment for students who "get it." Too often, students who excel in mathematics are not provided the same amount of time in a small-group setting. While it is tempting to structure small-group rotations to favor students who struggle, we must address the learning needs of all students. Consider students who excel with adding and subtracting fractions with unlike denominators. How can you enrich these students' learning? Students who are able to successfully add and subtract fractions with unlike denominators might have only one method they rely on when solving these problems. Asking these students to compute in more than one way or to interpret another student's solution strategy will afford them opportunities to understand the concept on a deeper level. A teacher can accommodate these students in a small group because he or she has the opportunity to take a close look at the students' strategies and ask them targeted probing questions to extend their thinking. These opportunities are often missed during whole-class instruction, as it is difficult to examine the thinking of each and every student in that setting.

Throughout this book, you will see examples of small-group instruction serving as both intervention and enrichment for different students. You might even see them occurring simultaneously as one student's learning is remediated while another student's learning is enriched.

The Importance of Making Sense of Mathematics for Teaching

We recognize that changing your teaching strategies or even your perspective on how best to teach mathematics in a small group is a challenging endeavor. Much of your work during small-group instruction consists of choosing appropriate tasks, supporting those tasks during instruction, engaging students in productive discourse, and collecting evidence to support decision making during instruction and for the instruction to come. Each of these aspects of planning and implementation requires content knowledge for teaching mathematics. As a result, if you have not already done so, we invite you to make sense of mathematics for teaching in general as you make sense of mathematics for teaching the pulled small group. Two helpful resources are *Making Sense of Mathematics for Teaching Grades K–2* (Dixon, Nolan, Adams, Brooks, & Howse, 2016) and *Making Sense of Mathematics for Teaching Grades 3–5* (Dixon, Nolan, Adams, Tobias, & Barmoha, 2016). We refer to these resources throughout the book. We strongly encourage you to read the grade-band book most relevant to your teaching role so that you gain the deep understanding of mathematics necessary to foster your ability to give students meaningful mathematics experiences in the pulled small group setting.

About This Book

Perhaps you are new to exploring the idea of implementing small-group instruction for mathematics. On the other hand, you may have been using this structure for years. Either way, your experiences will likely influence how you relate to the concepts presented in this book. We encourage you to take your time reading and implementing strategies as you encounter them. Consider reading with a colleague or in a collaborative team so you can share the journey and reflect on how these strategies impact student learning. We provide support through videos of authentic small-group instruction with students in kindergarten through grade 5. These videos, shared using Quick Response (QR) codes throughout the book, provide examples of best practices and help create a shared image of effective small-group instruction. The discussions following the videos will help you focus on key aspects of each lesson as they relate to the topics discussed in each respective chapter.

In chapter 1, you will gain insights into best practices for small-group instruction. You will learn how to effectively implement small-group instruction, and you will learn why each instructional practice presented is important for student learning. Chapter 2 focuses on the use of tasks, questions, and evidence (what we call the *TQE process*) for planning and implementing small-group instruction. You will have the opportunity to make sense of how tasks should connect to the learning goal, how you can use questions to uncover common errors, and how you can collect evidence during small-group instruction within a formative assessment process. Chapter 3 is focused on productive discourse. We share strategies to engage students in meaningful conversations and active participation related to mathematics during small-group instruction. Throughout the chapter, we will draw your attention to who is doing most of the talking, as well as to the mathematical quality of that talk. You will gain new understandings of effective small-group practices by exploring the establishment and maintenance of norms that create a shared ownership of learning. Finally, the epilogue concludes your exploration of small-group instruction with a synthesis of and reflection on key aspects of effective strategies. You'll have an opportunity to revisit the key aspects from each of the chapters as you view two more classroom videos. By this point, as you watch best practices in action, you will be well on your way to building a new framework for thinking about how you can effectively use small groups for mathematics instruction.

We recognize that it is much more common to see pulled-small-group instruction incorporated in elementary school settings. For this reason, our examples are provided within that setting as well. Those with a focus on secondary mathematics instruction can generalize these practices to their corresponding settings. And, while our focus is on effective strategies for teachers working with small groups of students, the strategies we suggest are appropriate for working with students one on one and in whole-group settings as well.

Throughout this book, we will use different icons to call your attention to various tasks to think about or perform. The *play button* icon, depicted in figure I.1 (page 6), indicates that an online video depicting a small-group lesson is available for you to watch. You can find the videos either by scanning the adjacent

Figure I.1: Play button icon.

Figure I.2: Task icon.

QR code or by following the provided URL. The *task* icon, in figure I.2, highlights academic tasks or problems featured in the videos. We encourage you to consider the tasks and how you might solve them, or help your students solve them, prior to watching the videos. We strongly recommend that you watch each video as you read this text to allow you to more fully understand the implementation and impact of each strategy suggested in this book.

Before reading on, use the following QR code to watch a video of author Juli Dixon sharing our perspectives related to best practices in small-group instruction. As you watch the video, think of how your current perspective on small-group instruction is similar to and different from Juli's perspective. You will have continued opportunities to reflect on using the TQE process and supporting productive discourse throughout the book. Our hope is that you are as excited to learn about small-group instruction as we are to share it. We will begin with an exploration of best practices.

Interview With Author Juli Dixon:
SolutionTree.com/DixonInterview

CHAPTER 1

Best Practices in Small-Group Instruction

Most of the elementary educators we have worked with view small-group instruction as an essential part of their mathematics block. Why? What are the benefits of small-group instruction that make it a priority in the school day? Typically, teachers consider it essential because they believe that they can fill gaps in student learning and meet students' individual needs during this time. However, based on a wealth of research on effective mathematics education, we can assume that small-group instruction that is focused solely on correcting errors in procedural computations rarely serves its intended purpose (NCTM, 2014).

In this chapter, we explore best practices and effective strategies for working with small groups, and we discuss how teachers can use the time as a powerful means to advance and deepen mathematical understanding for each and every learner, including those who have met the initial learning goal. We begin by analyzing a video that depicts several best practices for small-group mathematics instruction in the classroom, allowing you to consider the lesson's learning goal, the roles of the teacher and students, and the tools the teacher uses to support learning. Throughout the chapter we will discuss the teacher's role, effective teaching strategies, the students' roles, and how the teacher can help students negotiate those roles. We conclude by discussing management of the pulled small group.

Best Practices for Small Groups

According to *Principles to Actions*, "Effective teaching of mathematics engages students in solving and discussing tasks that promote mathematical reasoning and problem solving and allow multiple entry points and varied solution strategies" (NCTM, 2014, p. 17). Although best teaching practices that engage students in these behaviors, such as those described throughout this chapter, are becoming more common during whole-class instruction in mathematics, the same does not necessarily hold true during small-group instruction in mathematics. You likely do not need to stretch your memory too far to recall a class you observed or taught where both whole-class and small-group instruction was in place. Think about the sorts of mathematical experiences students encountered in the whole-class portion of the lesson compared to what they encountered in the pulled small group. The small-group portion of the lesson likely involved a teacher explaining a problem, directing the students to attempt the next problem on their own, then stepping in to provide scaffolding as the students struggle. This approach is much less grounded in reasoning and sense making than typical whole-class lessons.

During our work providing professional development and then observing the teachers following this work, we noticed that the best practices that professional development and professional articles are establishing regarding teaching and learning mathematics in whole-class instruction do not necessarily transfer to pulled-small-group instruction. The teachers often demonstrated growth in their whole-class instruction related to the professional development; however, when they pulled small groups of students, the teachers seemed to revert back to more traditional teaching practices.

You can likely relate to the frustration that stems from having provided information to students in a small-group setting only to have them seemingly forget it all the first moment they are expected to implement it on their own. What happens when instruction is limited to "teaching by telling"? Can you anticipate how instructional strategies based on transferring information to students may not be helpful for long-term understanding?

Now, in contrast to the preceding scenario, let's consider how we can build a new, shared image of what small-group instruction can accomplish. Consider the video of the grade 2 lesson Add Three-Digit Numbers With Regrouping using the following link or QR code. As you watch the video, make note of the difference between the typical small-group instructional model we just described and the lesson shared in the video. Use figure 1.1 to guide your observations as you watch the video. Be sure to watch the video before you continue reading.

    Add Three-Digit Numbers With Regrouping:
SolutionTree.com/GR2ThreeDigit

- What is the learning goal in this lesson?
- What is the teacher's role in this lesson?
- What are the students' roles?
- Which tools does the teacher provide to the students?
- What type of grouping does this small-group lesson use?
- In what ways does the teacher support the students to reason about the mathematics?

Figure 1.1: Guiding questions for observing best practices in small-group instruction.

In this lesson on multidigit addition, students are presented with the problem provided in figure 1.2 and asked to solve it individually. Please consider how you might approach this task before reading further.

Task

The candy shop at Sweet Tooth Elementary School has 376 candies. If the school orders another 258 candies, how much will the store have then?

Figure 1.2: Multidigit addition task.

Once the students are presented with the task, the teacher provides them with time to process the problem and work on their own. This allows students the opportunity to think critically about the mathematics and develop personal solution strategies. By observing the students as they start the solution process without interjecting or providing scaffolding, the teacher is able to use the task as part of a formative assessment process and gather evidence of students' current levels of understanding. She monitors the students to ensure they are engaging in a productive struggle and provides scaffolding or support if the struggle becomes unproductive (we cover productive and unproductive struggle in more depth on page 19). This balance is an important element of encouraging perseverance in each and every learner. By finding this balance between productive struggle and scaffolding, the teacher is fulfilling her role as a facilitator of learning.

Part of serving as a facilitator means providing students with resources and tools to reason about the mathematics. In this lesson, the teacher gives each student the option of using base ten blocks or whiteboards. By providing these tools, she ensures all students have access or an entry point to solving the problem in a way that works best for them. The students' role is to use their prior knowledge about addition, and what is provided to them, to work diligently to solve the problem. In this video, you see two students using base ten blocks and two students using an algorithm on the whiteboards to add the candy.

After observing the students working, the teacher engages one pair of students by asking, "What are you guys doing?" This simple question gives her an entry point into understanding the students' thinking. As Katie, the student in the peach shirt, explains how she used the algorithm to add, the teacher uses this contribution to reinforce place value language and understanding. Katie describes how she solved the problem by showing the teacher each step in the algorithm. The teacher questions Katie by referring to the 1 she recorded over the tens column in her algorithm and asks, "Is that a 1?" She crafts her question with the purpose of supporting Katie in making the connection between place value concepts and the algorithm—the learning goal for the lesson. The teacher's question also encourages the use of formal mathematical terminology, an important component of Mathematical Practice 6, "Attend to precision." Katie seems to experience difficulty making this connection, but the boy next to her, Marcus, chimes in, sharing that the 1 represents tens. Still focusing on developing Katie's understanding of place value in the algorithm, the teacher asks her to explain her peer's thinking. The teacher is encouraging Katie to make sense of Marcus's thinking.

The teacher continues to reinforce conceptual understanding of regrouping through the use of base ten blocks. She supports Katie in modeling the addition of 6 ones and 8 ones. Katie sees how 10 ones are regrouped into 1 ten. Once she demonstrates an understanding of place value language, the teacher asks Katie to turn to her partner and make sense of the rest of the algorithm using the base ten blocks. In this interaction, you see the teacher step in and provide just-in-time scaffolding (which we will discuss later in this chapter on page 11) to advance the students' conceptual understanding of the algorithm. You then see her pull back and encourage the students to continue to do the thinking and sense making. The action of pulling out of their conversation, rather than providing additional scaffolding just in case the students might need it, gives students an opportunity to return to engaging in a productive struggle.

Now that the teacher has supported one pair of students, she asks the other two students to explain their solution. Alejandro, the student in the red striped shirt, is doing all the talking, so the teacher asks his partner, Angela, to enter the conversation by saying, "Then what happened, Angela? What did you do with that 14?" All students must be held accountable for reasoning about the mathematics in a small-group setting. Angela is struggling with understanding how to connect place value language with base ten blocks. This is a common challenge for students. They are able to make sense of solving problems with manipulatives, and they also know how to use algorithms. The issue is that they do not make the connection between the two. Without the connection, they do not find the algorithm meaningful; rather, they just memorize it. Facilitating students to make this connection is an important role for the teacher, especially in a small group where the teacher can readily observe each student making connections and support the students when they fail to make needed connections. Because Angela's partner shows confidence with the mathematics, the teacher asks the pair to talk to each other about the last part of the solution. She uses peer talk as a support for deepening student understanding. In both pairs, you see the students working together to move their learning and understanding forward.

The teacher leaves the second pair of students to re-engage in their productive struggle and returns to the first pair to check on their progress. Katie is able to explain the algorithm with place value language, and the teacher reinforces the importance of using academic vocabulary by saying, "I like your language." The teacher brings the lesson to a close by supporting the students to describe how the base ten blocks and the algorithm are related. This connection is crucial in developing understanding as well as proficiency with regrouping. To proficiently use the algorithm, students need to make sense of the procedure. By asking students to connect a tool—in this case, the base ten blocks—with the algorithm, the teacher helps the students gain a deeper understanding of what the numbers in the algorithm represent, both with place value concepts and in the context of the candy shop problem.

It is likely that the video of small-group instruction you just watched has provided you with a different perspective on how to support students within a small-group setting. One aspect of the video that likely stood out is the role of the teacher. In order to use best teaching practices during pulled-small-group instruction, it is necessary to reconsider the teacher's role within the small group. The following section will introduce several strategies teachers may use to optimize small-group instruction.

The Teacher's Role in Small-Group Instruction

Recall the previously mentioned statement from *Principles to Actions* describing the role and purpose of a mathematics teacher: "Effective teaching of mathematics engages students in solving and discussing tasks that promote mathematical reasoning and problem solving and allow multiple entry points and varied solution strategies" (NCTM, 2014, p. 17). As the facilitator of a small group, a teacher may draw on several strategies in which to engage students, stimulate thinking and understanding, and encourage methods of problem solving. We present six teaching strategies that represent such best practices.

1. Delivering scaffolding

2. Providing accommodations

3. Enabling deeper understanding

4. Promoting layers of facilitation

5. Making use of the formative assessment process

6. Supporting perseverance

Although some of these strategies may be familiar to you, the ways in which we suggest teachers use them might challenge your current understanding of them, particularly for small-group instruction.

Implementing the strategies as recommended has the potential to positively change student engagement in mathematics within the small group.

Delivering Scaffolding

As you already observed in the video lesson (page 8), part of facilitating small-group instruction requires the teacher to provide support to students as needed. *Scaffolding* refers to providing tailored supports for students based on their current level of understanding in the learning progression, with the ultimate goal of advancing their learning along the progression. In this section, we will define what just-in-time scaffolding and additional methods of scaffolding entail.

Just-in-Time Scaffolding

Because teachers so often view pulled-small-group instruction as an opportunity for intervention, they tend to show the small group of students a strategy they can apply to solve a task before providing them with the time to discover strategies for solving the task on their own. This is an example of *just-in-case scaffolding*. Teachers so desperately want their students to succeed that they sometimes fall into the trap of doing the work, and the thinking, for their students. However, as tempting as it is to show students how to perform the mathematics before releasing them to try it on their own so they do not have to struggle, it is imperative that teachers allow all learners, including those who struggle, to make sense of and reason about the mathematics on their own first. This is a critical element of instruction in both whole-class and small-group environments. As mathematics educators Maggie B. McGatha and Jennifer M. Bay-Williams (2013) state, "For mathematics instruction to be truly meaningful and lasting, we have to support students in building on their own understanding and making connections among mathematical ideas" (p. 169). Students will build this understanding only if they have time to productively struggle with the mathematical ideas. Teachers may find it difficult to sit back and allow students the time they need to engage in a productive struggle. This can be especially difficult in small groups because the teacher witnesses students struggling at close range.

It is the teacher's role to provide scaffolding, including during small-group instruction. However, rather than taking a just-in-case approach, teachers need to provide this scaffolding just in time to support students to make sense of the mathematics, make connections, and engage in a productive struggle. By encouraging students to problem solve and reason about the mathematics, teachers are able to see what students already know. Once teachers have a clear idea of what students understand and what they have yet to understand, they can make the scaffolding much more precise and targeted to students' needs. Providing just-in-time scaffolding is a more effective method for filling in gaps in student learning than providing just-in-case scaffolding.

Additional Methods of Scaffolding

Although we suggest that scaffolding should be provided just in time, there are multiple ways to implement this just-in-time approach to scaffold student learning.

- Prompt students to explain their thinking.
- Clarify what the task is asking students to find.

- Clarify what prerequisite skills students already have or know.
- Allow students to explain their understanding with everyday language, and support them in re-voicing their thinking with academic vocabulary.
- Remind students to think of strategies they have seen or used in the past.
- Encourage students to collaborate with peers.

Using prompts and questions to have students explain their thinking forces them to take a closer look at their thought processes. Many times, just by explaining their thinking, students realize their own errors. Teachers can also use prompts or questions to clarify for students what a task is asking. If students are struggling, they may lack clarity on what the task is asking them to find. Rereading the task and focusing on students' interpretations of the implied meaning will support them in analyzing and using the appropriate information. For example, in this chapter we will show a lesson featuring the following task.

> You have 384 packaged candies. How would you
> distribute them evenly on 4 shelves?

A student might initially struggle with this task because they are unclear on what the word *distribute* means. Clarifying the meaning of this word by offering a synonym or description will help the student comprehend what the task is asking.

Asking students to reread the task in order to interpret its meaning is different from asking students to rely on key words. Reliance on key words or phrases, such as *fewer*, *how many more*, and *altogether*, can lead to confusion and ultimately poor performance in mathematics. This practice is strongly discouraged (you can read more about key words and the dangers of using them in chapter 2 of *Making Sense of Mathematics for Teaching Grades K–2* [Dixon, Nolan, Adams, Brooks, & Howse, 2016]). However, in some cases, when students struggle with the words presented in mathematical concepts or tasks as these concepts are first introduced, suggesting that students use everyday language to describe the new concepts or tasks is an excellent strategy. Teachers can also use this strategy as a scaffolding technique when students struggle. But eventually, it will be useful to home in on the academic language to help students make sense of the problem. Focusing on academic language to help students understand a task is different from focusing on key words as a quick trick to help students solve the task.

When students do not know how to begin solving a task, teachers have a choice regarding how they will respond. They can provide a prompt or a cue. When they *prompt* students' thinking they assist students in identifying the various strategies they can try. For example, a teacher may say, "Think about strategies you have used or seen used in the past," to help students recall different strategies that might be applicable to solving the task. This type of prompt supports students in developing their problem-solving skills while still leaving the ownership for critical thinking on the students. If students are still stuck, teachers can *cue* them by naming a specific strategy to try. This type of cue, such as "Try drawing a bar model," will provide struggling students with an entry point for solving the problem. Because a cue takes some of the ownership and cognitive demand off students, we recommend using a prompt before providing a cue.

In addition to providing support through teacher-to-student prompting and cueing, teachers can encourage student-to-student questioning and discussion. (You will read more about the types of questions teachers can ask to advance student discourse in chapters 2 and 3 [pages 31 and 49].) Having students collaborate and work with peers on a concept they are struggling with is another great way to scaffold. Students learn from thinking through new concepts with peers. Heterogeneous, or mixed-ability, grouping within the small group sets the stage for students to collaborate effectively with their peers. This aspect of small-group instruction is described in greater detail later in this chapter (see page 23).

Providing Accommodations

Accommodations differ from scaffolding in that scaffolding relates to supporting students' current understanding of a particular concept or topic, whereas accommodations are pre-set, tailored support for students based on their overall instructional needs. For example, a student who is visually impaired will need the accommodation of having larger print or more verbal directions. This accommodation ensures the student has access to the content. For this reason, accommodations should be considered and planned in advance, or "just in case." However, if this same student is struggling with addition, the teacher might provide just-in-time scaffolding through prompting, or even cueing, to help the student make connections between joining situations and the process of addition. Likewise, if students need a task read to them in order to engage in thinking about the task, then you need to accommodate them by reading the task to them. The students' struggle should occur while *reasoning* about the mathematics, not in *accessing* the task.

To help you interpret which situations require just-in-case accommodations versus just-in-case scaffolding, consider the scenario of teaching a toddler to brush her teeth. The toddler is not tall enough to reach the sink on her own. In order to allow her to access the sink, her caregiver will need to provide her with a step stool. Providing her with the step stool is an example of an appropriate just-in-case accommodation. This accommodation is necessary because without it, the toddler would have no chance of succeeding in brushing her teeth. With the step stool, the toddler can reach the sink, and she is ready to begin brushing her teeth. An example of inappropriate just-in-case scaffolding would occur if each time the toddler brushed her teeth, the caregiver did the brushing for her; then, she might end up becoming a teenager who still needs an adult to brush her teeth. Instead, the caregiver allows the toddler to brush her teeth herself and provides her with feedback and support along the way.

It is also important to know the difference between just-in-case scaffolding and just-in-time scaffolding. Just-in-time scaffolding is preferrable. If the caregiver notices the toddler isn't reaching the teeth in the back of her mouth, the caregiver will help her by either reminding her or modeling it for her. This example of just-in-time scaffolding gives the toddler the opportunity to practice brushing her teeth while the caregiver acts as a guide to monitor her behavior and ensure her success.

Enabling Deeper Understanding

In addition to providing scaffolding and accommodations in small-group instruction, a component of being a facilitator of student learning is helping students gain a deep understanding of mathematical topics. Deep understanding requires a balance of conceptual understanding, procedural skill, and procedural fluency. In *Taking Action: Implementing Effective Mathematics Teaching Practices in K–Grade 5*, professors DeAnn Huinker and Victoria Bill (2017) discuss the importance of building deep conceptual understanding of mathematics at the elementary level. During the early years, students establish their initial mathematical understandings on which all later learning will be built. If this process is rushed and students are not granted the opportunity to understand the *why* of mathematics, you risk students losing confidence in their ability to *do* mathematics, as well as their understanding that mathematical ideas are connected. When students learn mathematics as a set of procedures, then they view mathematics as separate pieces of knowledge to memorize, rather than a connected discipline to understand and apply. Teachers have the power to promote mathematics as a coherent discipline or to leave students to believe that mathematics does not make sense.

As you saw in the video Add Three-Digit Numbers With Regrouping (page 8), focusing on conceptual understanding first led to a deeper understanding of a standard algorithm for multidigit addition. Table 1.1 shows teacher actions that support teaching mathematics for understanding and teacher actions that inhibit the development of this understanding during small-group instruction.

Table 1.1: Teacher Actions to Promote and Avoid During Small-Group Instruction

Teacher Actions to Promote	Teacher Actions to Avoid
<ul><li>Selecting appropriate tasks</li><li>Evaluating and monitoring student understanding</li><li>Asking questions to address common errors</li><li>Asking questions to advance student thinking</li><li>Providing support and scaffolding as needed</li></ul>	<ul><li>Showing students a strategy *before* giving them time to solve the task on their own</li><li>Telling students whether they are correct or incorrect without allowing them to reason collaboratively</li><li>Providing scaffolding just in case students might need it</li></ul>

Promoting Layers of Facilitation

How to deliver content during small-group instruction is one of many pivotal decisions that enable students to think critically about mathematics. As mentioned in the introduction (page 1), an instructional model that has become common in many schools and that teachers often incorporate into small-group instruction is the gradual release of responsibility model of "I do, we do, you do" (Fisher & Frey, 2014). Although the gradual release of responsibility is appropriate at times, such as when introducing a procedure, the model needs to change when the goal is to have students explore concepts or make connections among concepts and procedures. For such goals, teaching strategies should allow students to do the sense making and reasoning associated with the concepts. This shift makes way for the development of meaning related to concepts. *Layers of facilitation* is a student-centered instructional method that promotes critical thinking and problem solving (Dixon, Nolan, Adams, Brooks, & Howse, 2016; Dixon, Nolan, Adams, Tobias, & Barmoha, 2016). Facilitation consists of three layers, each from the teacher's perspective.

1. I *facilitate the whole class* to engage in meaningful tasks through questioning.

2. I *facilitate small groups* to extend the learning initiated in the whole-group setting.

3. I *facilitate individuals* to provide evidence of their understanding of the learning goal.

"This change in teacher role focuses on the teacher as a facilitator of knowledge acquisition rather than as a transmitter of knowledge" (Dixon, Nolan, Adams, Brooks, & Howse, 2016, p. 10). In this instructional approach, the teacher sets up concurrent small groups of students who will work together on the task provided. Concurrent small groups are different from pulled small groups in that concurrent small groups each work on the same shared mathematics task at the same time. During concurrent small-group time, the teacher circulates from group to group to facilitate students' thinking while students work collaboratively within their group setting. In contrast, a pulled small group occurs when the teacher works with one group of students while the rest of the class is engaged in different instructional activities, such as in centers or on independent work.

So where does small-group instruction fit into the layers of facilitation? The teacher can pull a small group during the third layer of facilitation, while other students work independently or in centers. In this way, the pulled small group addresses the content that the teacher first introduced in a whole-class discussion. The objective of this small group might be to engage in a task that goes deeper than the original lesson, or perhaps the purpose is to engage in a task that revisits the original concept if students struggled with certain aspects of that concept. It is important to hold students individually accountable for reasoning about the mathematics within each lesson through the third layer of facilitation.

As a teacher or administrator, think about how your current structure and expectation for the mathematics block allows you to strategically use small-group instruction. A common belief among educators is that time must be set aside daily for pulled-small-group instruction. However, some lessons may span multiple instructional blocks or days. When viewed in this way, the first two layers of facilitation might occur on the first day of the lesson, and the teacher might pull a small group during the third layer of facilitation on the second day of the lesson. How much time you should spend in small-group instruction depends on the evidence of student learning collected during the formative assessment process (see the following section, Making Use of the Formative Assessment Process). As a result, when planning small-group instruction, teachers must carefully consider time management. Although time spent in the small group can be beneficial, it is important to recognize that it can also detract from the work of the whole class. Students who are not included in the pulled small group work in centers, which might not be academically engaging. This frequently leaves these students at risk of engaging in off-task behavior. We'll address considerations for establishing meaningful centers later in this chapter (page 28).

Although a teacher might pull a small group during the third layer of facilitation, the small group can be thought of as a microcosm of the entire classroom, where the structure of the layers of facilitation is used in its entirety. The teacher engages the whole small group in a meaningful task and then facilitates partners and individuals to extend their understanding and provide evidence of their learning. This structure is evident in the Add Three-Digit Numbers With Regrouping video lesson (page 8) you viewed previously. An important aspect of the layers of facilitation, regardless of how it applies to the small group, is that the teacher's role shifts from provider of information to facilitator of student understanding. This has implications for how the teacher applies the formative assessment process.

Making Use of the Formative Assessment Process

In order to facilitate students to make connections between and deepen their understandings of mathematical concepts, you must remain acutely aware of what the students understand and what common errors they make. This requires a constant formative assessment process. Language around formative assessment is common in education literature; however, definitions of the term *formative assessment* vary (Wiliam, 2018). According to education consultant Dylan Wiliam (2018):

> An assessment functions formatively to the extent that evidence about student achievement is elicited, interpreted, and used by teachers, learners, or their peers to make decisions about the next steps in instruction that are likely to be better, or better founded, than the decisions they would have made in the absence of that evidence. (p. 48)

The formative assessment process is what allows teachers to provide necessary, individualized support to their students. Teachers should use it to collect data for determining whom they should pull into the small group, as well as to deepen student understanding during small-group instructional time. To engage in the formative assessment process, a teacher does not need to develop an additional task. Rather, the formative assessment process should occur throughout the small-group lesson. The teacher uses the task or concept he or she asks students to reason about within the small group both as part of the formative assessment process and as an instructional opportunity.

Assessment is a vital part of the instructional process. As students are engaging in the task, the teacher gathers evidence of students' understanding by observing their behavior and asking questions. However, if the teacher provides just-in-case scaffolding, then formative assessment is not embedded in the learning process. If you show students how to think before you observe how they think independently, then you will not gain any new data on their level of understanding. At that point, you are simply monitoring how well they can replicate a procedure or skill you just showed them. A task within a lesson can serve as a tool for collecting evidence within the formative assessment process when you provide students with opportunities to show what they know. How do *you* gauge student understanding during small-group instruction? This is an important question to discuss with your collaborative team.

Consider the following grade 5 division problem through a candy shop context (see figure 1.3). Take a moment to solve this problem using two different strategies before you continue reading. Think about how you'd gauge students' understanding if they were solving it.

Task

You have 384 packaged candies. How would you distribute them evenly on 4 shelves?

Figure 1.3: Division task.

How did you solve the problem? Did your strategies support the context of the problem? There are two types of division contexts: (1) sharing and (2) measurement. In a division problem, the total is known, and either the number of groups or the number of objects in each group is unknown. When both the total and the number of groups are known, the problem represents a sharing, or *partitive*, division context. The task in figure 1.3 provides the total amount of candy and the number of groups, or shelves, the candy needs to be shared among. Therefore, the total and the number of groups are known, making this problem an example of sharing division. If the total and the number of objects in each group were both known, then the problem would be an example of measurement division.

Did you use the long division algorithm to solve the problem? To interpret the meaning of the long division algorithm, you should model the sharing context. However, it is typical that the language we use to describe the procedure for this algorithm is void of meaning because it instead represents measurement division. The first step often begins with the question, "How many times does 4 go into 38?" There are many issues with this language that fall beyond the scope of this book (see chapter 2 of *Making Sense of Mathematics for Teaching Grades 3–5* [Dixon, Nolan, Adams, Tobias, & Barmoha, 2016] for an in-depth discussion of division). However, what is important to realize here is that the language of this question mirrors measurement division, because it seeks to determine the number of groups of four there are in 384, rather than sharing division, where you would seek to determine how many candies would be in each of four groups. The video that follows addresses the language you would use when a problem represents a sharing division context. Please watch the video of the grade 5 lesson Make Sense of the Long Division Algorithm before you continue reading. As you watch this video, reflect on the following questions provided in figure 1.4.

Make Sense of the Long Division Algorithm:
SolutionTree.com/GR5LongDivision

- What evidence of the formative assessment process do you see in the video?
- In what ways does the teacher use best practices during small-group instruction?
- In what ways do the students participate within the pulled small group?
- How does the teacher leverage students' conceptual understanding to make sense of an algorithm?
- How does the sharing division context support students in interpreting the meaning of the long division algorithm?

Figure 1.4: Guiding questions for observing roles in small-group instruction.

In this video, the teacher gives each pair of students a tool to provide them with an access point for solving the problem. In this situation, the most appropriate tool is a set of base ten blocks because they serve as a bridge for understanding the sharing model of division through place value. The teacher asks the students to make sense of the task by showing the 384 candies with their base ten blocks. She observes the students as they begin to represent sharing their candies evenly among the four shelves. How does this observation contribute to the formative assessment process? By watching the students demonstrate division, the teacher notices the students are struggling. She realizes the students are dividing the candy into groups of four instead of into four groups. Now that she has these formative assessment data of student understanding, she uses this information to formulate her next step. The teacher prompts the first pair of students, Jordana and Juliana, by asking them to explain what they are doing. This prompt encourages the students to reason aloud and catch their own misunderstandings. The girl in gray, Juliana, even says,

"Oh," at this realization. Jordana and Juliana realize they are representing the context of the problem by dividing the candy into groups of four instead of into four groups. It isn't until after the teacher notices the students dividing the candy incorrectly that she scaffolds their learning by questioning their strategy. It is important that the teacher provides the opportunity for students to begin with their own thinking. Choosing to ask students to explain their thinking when she sees they've made an error is an example of just-in-time, rather than just-in-case, scaffolding.

In addition to providing scaffolding through her questioning, the teacher scaffolds student learning through facilitating student-to-student discourse. The teacher leverages Jordana's and Juliana's newfound understanding by asking them to watch what the other pair of students do and offer assistance. She places the ownership of learning on the students. They adhere to their roles by explaining their thinking. Listening to their peers' thinking helps the second pair of students, Julio and Jayda, realize that the candy shop context is an example of sharing division, as opposed to measurement division. Within the small-group instruction, the teacher acts as a facilitator and supports students to make sense of the mathematics.

Part of the facilitative role of the teacher involves intentionally developing learning progressions to support students' learning of concepts before procedures. Gaining a deep understanding of a concept enables students to justify the steps within a procedure so they are less likely to incorrectly use the procedure. In this video, you see how teachers can allow students to make sense of standard algorithms through the use of context and tools. How does the candy shop context help the students make sense of the long division algorithm? The sharing context created by the candy shop task, coupled with the place value understanding the students develop through the use of the base ten blocks, provides the students with language for explaining the long division algorithm. The teacher encourages the students to explain the long division algorithm by using the base ten blocks and the sharing language present in the candy shop context. She takes advantage of the size of the small group by providing each student with an opportunity to express one step of the standard algorithm. When Juliana begins to explain the solution process using the long division algorithm, she reverts to using "goes into" language. This language describes the steps of the long division algorithm in a procedural, rather than conceptual, way; the verbiage does not refer to the base ten place value system in a meaningful way. What does it mean when she says, "Four goes into 3"? The teacher initiates connections to place value understanding by asking Juliana what the 3 and 4 represent in the candy shop context. In this way, she is avoiding the meaningless "goes into" language and replacing it with a meaningful connection that bridges the steps of the algorithm to the concepts behind them.

As the teacher continues to prompt student thinking by referring back to the context, the students become more comfortable using place value language to describe the steps in the algorithm. The teacher is helping the students develop formal mathematical terminology, which aligns to Mathematical Practice 6, "Attend to precision." She is also helping students make sense of the mathematical structure inherent in the long division algorithm as she supports students to connect their understanding of dividing with base ten blocks to the written algorithm. She supports students to engage in Mathematical Practice 7, "Look for and make use of structure." Within the small-group setting, all students are held accountable for demonstrating their new learning when their turn comes to continue explaining the long division algorithm.

Supporting Perseverance

Mathematical Practice 1, "Make sense of problems and persevere in solving them," requires students to become problem solvers who feel comfortable trying new strategies and who can adjust when a strategy does not work. Perseverance and resilience within mathematics do not automatically come to all students. You need to support your students as they develop these essential characteristics. How can you encourage students to persevere in problem solving while avoiding their feelings of frustration and urges to give up? By allowing students to productively struggle with a mathematics task, you are assisting them in developing problem-solving skills. The pulled small group provides an excellent structure for this but only if you are careful with how and when you provide support.

You may think that your job, when teaching students, is to make concepts easier and therefore more attainable. This, in turn, leads you to think that when students are not immediately successful, you have failed them. When this happens, you may instinctively jump in to "save" students by walking them through each step in the problem-solving process. This instinct is even more prevalent when teachers see an administrator in the room, because they want to show the administrator that their instruction is leading to student success. Even though your goal in acting on these instincts is to help students, it will unintentionally result in lowering the cognitive demand of the task, and students will no longer have the opportunity to reason about the mathematics. In fact, if you retire your superhero cape and provide the space for students to work, it is likely that it will empower them and they will flourish in their effort to think critically. We encourage teachers and administrators to speak about their expectations for productive struggle and the development of problem-solving strategies in the mathematics classroom.

So what does productive struggle look like, and how do you support it? To understand *productive* struggle, you must first understand *unproductive* struggle. A student experiencing unproductive struggle has reached a point of frustration. The student is likely to give up on the task and shut down. The student might feel hopeless and incapable of reaching the learning goal—maybe the task is inaccessible to the student as presented. On the other hand, a student experiencing productive struggle feels hopeful about solving the problem. This student is thinking back to various strategies he or she has used in the past to find one that will work in this scenario. Productive struggle leads to a sense of pride, ownership of learning, and mathematical understanding.

Anticipating common errors will help you prepare scaffolds and supports to avoid feelings of frustration. However, you must take care to provide these scaffolds just in time rather than just in case. Some strategies for engaging students in productive struggle include the following.

- Use open-ended tasks that allow for multiple entry points and solution strategies.

- Provide students with tools that will support them in reasoning about the mathematics.

- Structure the small-group environment to promote student collaboration.

- Praise students for their effort and thinking.

- Provide students with feedback on their reasoning.

- Anticipate common errors, and prepare for them in advance.

To engage students in productive struggle, present them with open-ended tasks that have multiple entry points and solution strategies. Allowing students to choose their own approach gives them an opportunity to make connections to previously learned concepts or material. Another strategy that supports a productive struggle is to provide students access to tools that will assist them in thinking about the mathematics (NCTM, 2014). In addition to providing access to appropriate tools, you can support a productive struggle through the setup of the classroom. As Huinker and Bill (2017) state, "Classroom environments that support productive struggle give students time and space to grapple individually with mathematical tasks, to work in pairs and small groups, and to engage in whole-class discussions" (p. 213). The teacher establishes such an environment within small-group instruction when he or she gives students the opportunity to make sense of problems and supports them to work collaboratively. The pulled small group is an excellent structure for supporting discussion and providing productive feedback.

As students are working on a cognitively demanding task, be careful regarding the feedback you provide. Positive reinforcement should validate students' work ethic and perseverance. When you praise students only for correct answers, they begin to see value only in getting the correct answer—not in the effort that goes into finding the answer or in the process used to achieve it. This type of praise that overemphasizes correct answers can lead to unproductive struggle and often makes students who do not get the correct answer feel frustrated. In addition to providing students feedback on their efforts, give them thoughtful feedback on their mathematical reasoning. When you give feedback on students' thinking, you are validating their thinking. Students will develop a sense of pride when reasoning about mathematics. The same result occurs when you ask questions that encourage students to explore their mathematical understandings on a deeper level. If you are careful with the feedback you offer, you can support students to develop perseverance.

The following video, Order and Compute With Coins, shows second-grade students engaging in a productive struggle within small-group instruction as they work through a missing addend money task. As you watch the video, use the questions in figure 1.5 to guide your thinking. Watch the video before you continue reading.

Order and Compute With Coins:
SolutionTree.com/GR2Coins

- What scaffolds does the teacher provide?
- What evidence of student struggle do you observe?
- How does the teacher engage different learning levels within the same small group?

Figure 1.5: Guiding questions for observing a lesson on a missing addend within the context of money.

The video begins with the teacher asking the students to make observations about the coins in their bin. This quick activity activates the students' prior knowledge and provides the teacher with evidence of the students' current knowledge of the coins. The teacher extends this activity by asking the students to order the coins from the coin with the least value to the coin with the greatest value. This allows the teacher to see that all but one student, Riley, have correctly ordered the coins. Instead of pointing out the error, the teacher uses this information in her formative assessment process and places the ownership for learning on the students. She does this by asking them to look at each other's coins to see whether they all have the same order. Because the students do not notice the one incorrect response, the teacher initiates the discussion by telling Riley, "Tell us about yours." Just by being asked to explain his solution, Riley quickly finds and corrects his error on his own. This teacher prompt serves as a scaffold for the student.

Once the teacher is confident the students know the value of each coin, she presents the students with a task. After reading the story problem aloud, she asks the students what they are trying to find out. This question allows the teacher to ensure students have clarity regarding the task. Lack of clarity regarding a task can lead to frustration, causing students' struggles to become unproductive. Because the learning goal is for students to determine a missing addend within the context of money, their productive struggle should center on doing the mathematics, not interpreting the word problem. In addition to ensuring all students understand the task, the teacher provides the students with a tool to support their learning—coins. In this story problem context, the coins serve as a manipulative and a support for making sense of the missing addend. They assist students in finding the solution to the task.

Before releasing the students to start working, the teacher prompts their thinking by asking, "How are you going to start?" Trace shares that he is going to start with a quarter. The teacher encourages other students to make sense of their peer's thinking by asking, "Why did he say he started with a quarter?" She then releases the students to begin solving the problem. One student, Carysa, does not engage with the task; she does not know how to start. To keep Carysa's struggle from becoming unproductive, the teacher provides just-in-time scaffolding. The teacher provides a cue in the form of rereading the first sentence, which gives the student a starting point with the task of displaying forty-three cents. Now that the teacher knows Carysa can begin working, she pulls her attention away from Carysa and provides scaffolding for another student, Grady. This dance of stepping in and stepping out of supporting a student is essential in giving each student an opportunity to productively struggle.

Grady has forty-three cents displayed in front of him, so the teacher prompts him to explain his thinking by asking, "What are you going to do next?" Grady has succeeded in completing the task, so the teacher challenges him by asking him to see whether he could have picked up a different set of coins. How does this extension question allow the teacher to differentiate instruction within the small group? Given his extension task, the student exclaims, "This is hard." The teacher now knows she has succeeded in providing the student with an extension so he also has an opportunity to productively struggle. Confident that this extension is of an appropriate level of challenge for him, the teacher encourages Grady to keep working to develop his perseverance.

Once Trace and Riley complete the task, the teacher has them explain to each other what they did and how they know they are right. This prompt provides an opportunity for these two students to learn from each other. At the end of the video, you see that although Carysa struggled in the beginning, she finds a solution. The teacher validates Carysa's hard work and supports her perseverance by asking her to explain her solution. This task allowed Carysa to work toward proficiency with Mathematical Practice 1, "Make sense of problems and persevere in solving them."

Now that we have discussed the teacher's role in small-group instruction and presented several teaching strategies, let's turn our attention to the role of the student.

The Students' Roles in Small-Group Instruction

As we previously discussed, it is the teacher's role to facilitate students in the process of reasoning and making sense of the mathematics within the pulled small group. Teachers do this through strategies such as using layers of facilitation, incorporating a formative assessment process, providing scaffolding, and supporting perseverance. It is also important to consider the role of the students during small-group instruction. Students need clear expectations regarding their role in the small group. Students should be active learners who reason about the content; they should demonstrate that they are engaged by asking questions and making connections. It is *not* the students' role to passively learn and only engage in the mathematics by acting in compliance with the teacher's requests to perform mathematical computations and procedures. The teacher must make explicit each student's role as an active learner during small-group instruction.

The Mathematical Practices provide a helpful structure for determining the expectations for students' engagement with the mathematics. For example, if the teacher wants the students to make sense of a procedure by looking at the solutions to several different but related problems, the teacher would be explicit about the students' role in looking for and using patterns. In this way, the teacher is supporting students to engage in Mathematical Practice 8, "Look for and express regularity in repeated reasoning." While we include some examples here, the types of questions you use to engage students in specific Mathematical Practices are discussed in detail in chapter 2 of this book (page 31).

Students must use what they already know about mathematics to connect new mathematics knowledge to existing knowledge. To make these connections, students should be risk takers. This is supported by engaging students in Mathematical Practice 1, "Make sense of problems and persevere in solving them." They should invent and try new strategies, including using drawings and other tools, to engage in Mathematical Practice 5, "Use appropriate tools strategically." Students should explain their thinking and listen to the thinking of their peers. If they do not understand their peers' reasoning, then they need to ask questions to gain clarity. This is an example of Mathematical Practice 3, "Construct viable arguments and critique the reasoning of others."

Students are accustomed to the teacher being the owner of knowledge during small-group instruction. To challenge this convention, McGatha and Bay-Williams (2013) describe creating a community of learners in which the mathematical authority belongs to the classroom of learners, not just the teacher. It is important that students understand there is not one owner of knowledge—every member of the community is a learner, including the teacher. Although the teacher may prompt the group to determine a response's validity, it is up to the students to participate in student-to-student discussion to determine the correctness of the reasoning or answer. This is accomplished by the tasks the teacher uses and the questions the teacher chooses to support those tasks. Chapter 2 (page 31) is focused on the process used to plan for these tasks and to implement them during small-group instruction.

If you show students the passion you have for learning and interpreting the mathematical world around them, they might also develop a passion for learning mathematics. How can you encourage students to own their learning in this manner? Establishing norms for discourse within small-group instruction can assist in setting expectations for student behaviors. We will explore establishing norms for small-group instruction in chapter 3 (page 49).

Now that we have established the roles for teachers and students and effective teaching strategies for small-group instruction, let's think about how to structure and manage time spent in the pulled small group.

Management of the Pulled Small Group

Although the term *classroom management* encompasses many aspects of classroom structure, it is typically thought of as relating to handling student behavior in the classroom. The purpose of this section is to address classroom management beyond notions of discipline; this section focuses on managing the structures in your classroom and pulled small group that can make learning more meaningful. There are several components to consider in regard to managing the pulled small group. In this section, we focus on grouping, instruction and differentiation, tools, and centers.

Grouping

How do you currently select students for small-group instruction? The composition of a small group sets the stage for the type of discussions that will occur within the small-group setting. It is not necessary to require small-group instruction every day for every student. Rather, you should base decisions for when to meet and whom to meet with in small groups on the needs of the students at any given time. The groupings should be fluid and grounded in the data collected during your formative assessment process.

The learning goal should also help you determine the type of grouping most appropriate for a lesson. There are advantages to both homogeneous and heterogeneous grouping. Homogeneous grouping allows the focus to be on filling a shared need among a group of students. This is particularly helpful if all students are struggling with a specific procedure and need guided support in practicing that procedure. Although homogeneous grouping may be appropriate when the focus is procedural, we advocate for selecting heterogeneous groups when the focus is on developing conceptual understanding or problem-solving strategies.

Within a heterogeneous group, each student brings a unique set of strengths and understandings to the table. According to mathematics education researchers Erna Yackel and Paul Cobb (1996), students have more opportunities to learn when they make sense of each other's thinking and compare different solution strategies to their own. You create opportunities for these rich conversations when you group students with different perspectives and levels of understanding. If a student is struggling with a mathematical concept, the student will benefit from listening to a peer share a unique understanding of the same concept. In addition, the peer who is sharing will benefit from having to put this understanding into words, because when students talk through a concept, they develop a deeper understanding of that concept (Dean, Hubbell, Pitler, & Stone, 2012). If all students in the group share the same level of understanding of a mathematical concept, including similar common errors, then the environment will not support mathematical debate and the creation of new understandings. Homogeneous grouping is typical for small-group instruction, and this practice needs to be examined and adjusted as necessary.

You and your collaborative team might benefit from a conversation related to how you group students during mathematics instruction.

The following video shows a heterogeneous group of grade 1 students deepening their understanding of measurement. Within this grade level, students are responsible for extending their understanding of direct comparison to an understanding of indirect comparison. If a student were to hold two pipe cleaners in his hands and determine which one was longer, then he would be using direct comparison to relate the objects' sizes. With indirect comparison, students compare the lengths of two objects by knowing how each object compares to a third object. In this video, the goal is for students to use indirect comparison. As you watch the video, reflect on how the heterogeneous grouping allows all students within the small group to advance and deepen their understanding of indirect comparison. Use the questions in figure 1.6 to guide your thoughts. Watch the video of the lesson Compare Objects Using Indirect Measurement before you continue reading.

Compare Objects Using Indirect Measurement:
SolutionTree.com/GR1CompareObjects

- How does the group's composition support student understanding of the mathematics?
- What evidence do you see of students learning from other students?
- How might this lesson have gone differently with a homogeneous group of students?

Figure 1.6: Guiding questions for observing heterogeneous grouping in small-group instruction.

In the beginning of the lesson, the teacher activates the students' prior knowledge of measuring the length of objects using direct measurement. Once she ensures that all the students in the group understand that in order to accurately measure the length of the pipe cleaner, they must lay the tiles end to end without gaps or overlaps, the teacher moves on to the next learning experience. This learning experience also serves as a means of collecting evidence of the students' prerequisite knowledge using the formative assessment process. She asks the students to measure the straw that she gives them, but she intentionally provides the students with fewer tiles than they need. Olivia states that the straw is three tiles long because she has only three tiles. The other students in the group correct this error through conversation around their solution strategies. While it is important to collect formative data related to prerequisite skills during the time in the pulled small group, it is also important to address the learning goal. How does the teacher transition to the learning goal—using indirect comparison? In what ways does she maintain the focus on the students for the sense-making activity?

Instead of showing the students how to use indirect measurement to compare objects, the teacher encourages the students to discover this method through the planned activity. She asks them to select an object from a pile of objects and determine whether the object is shorter or longer than the straw, which they already measured to be five tiles. Olivia is asked to go first and selects a magnifying glass, claiming it is shorter than the straw. The teacher provides an opportunity for Olivia to engage in Mathematical Practice 3, "Construct viable arguments and critique the reasoning of others," by asking her how she can prove her claim that the magnifying glass is shorter than five tiles. Olivia illustrates her thinking by measuring the magnifying glass with the tiles. Her classmate, Phoenix, suggests using the straw to compare the objects' lengths, but Olivia does not believe this is possible. Olivia's disbelief that she can compare the lengths in this manner is evidence that she might not be ready to use indirect comparison. How could you support this student in advancing her thinking?

Because the learning goal for the lesson is to use indirect comparison, the teacher intentionally selects Phoenix to pick an object next. Through prior discussion, the teacher is fairly confident that Phoenix will show the group how to use indirect measurement to compare the straw to his selected object and thereby determine whether his object is longer or shorter than five tiles. Not only does this enable all other students in the group to learn from the student who has achieved the learning goal, but it also provides an opportunity for Phoenix to explain his thinking and thus advance his own understanding. How does the grouping of the students influence opportunities for student-centered instruction?

Choosing a heterogeneous small group creates the opportunity for students to learn from one another. Facilitating student learning within the small group allows the teacher to take advantage of this situation. By intentionally sequencing the order in which she calls on students using information she collected within the formative assessment process, the teacher is planning for students to learn from one another. Some worry that heterogeneous small groups might not provide the more advanced students with worthwhile learning experiences. However, when students are required to verbally express their thinking, they gain a deeper command of the mathematical concepts. In this way, all students in the group have the opportunity to advance their understanding.

Instruction and Differentiation

Small-group instruction can be a powerful vehicle for differentiation. However, the way teachers often implement small-group instruction does not allow for productive differentiation. Productive differentiation is designed to provide students with experiences that connect with their specific levels of understanding, uncover common errors, and move learning forward. Students have varying learning needs. This variance cannot be accounted for when teachers instruct the entire group in the same way. Often, teachers view small-group instruction as a time to reteach students who are struggling with a mathematical topic. They typically restructure this reteaching in such a way that they show students how to perform the procedure and provide students with time to practice. However, when teachers expect all students to perform the mathematics in the same way, they likely do not address the students' individual needs.

According to University of Central Florida professors of education Gina Gresham and Mary Little (2012), to provide effective instruction based on students' individual needs, teachers must assess student learning by gauging how quickly and thoroughly a student attains a concept and then adapting their instruction according to what they have gathered about that student's learning. The teacher's role in productive differentiated instruction is to create the learning experience and facilitate student learning by providing students with individual supports and challenges as needed. This can and should occur during daily instruction. The learning is differentiated because, although all students are challenged with the same learning experience, the teacher provides them with unique supports based on their current level of understanding.

Reflect on the video you watched of students in grade 1 comparing objects with the goal of using indirect measurement. How did the teacher differentiate by providing unique supports? In the video, we see the students measuring the lengths of their straws using tiles. We see Olivia state that the straw is three tiles in length because she ran out of tiles to continue measuring. The teacher differentiates her support through the questions she asks each child. She asks Olivia why she said the straw was three tiles. Once Olivia shares her thinking, the teacher enriches the other students' understanding by providing them with the opportunity to share how they could measure even though they do not have enough tiles. Later in the video, Olivia is given the opportunity to compare the length of the magnifying glass with her straw. Since Olivia is not ready to compare with indirect measurement, the teacher allows her to explore her current thinking of using the tiles to measure and exposes her to the deeper understanding of her classmate, Phoenix.

Small-group instruction can provide the structure for productive differentiation when you use effective strategies during the small-group lesson. Effective instructional strategies include addressing student errors, providing opportunities for students to collaborate with their peers, encouraging students to speak and write about the mathematics, and presenting multiple representations of the content through the use of mathematical tools. What follows are some specific suggestions on how you can use tools to support student learning.

Tools

In the video of the grade 5 lesson Make Sense of the Long Division Algorithm (page 17), you saw students using base ten blocks to find a solution to the task. They manipulated the tool to evenly share the candy among the four shelves. However, you also saw the students using the tool to make sense of the task. At first, the students were making groups of four, instead of sharing among four groups. They realized that to match the context of the problem, they needed to use the base ten blocks differently and share among the four shelves, instead of making groups of four candies. In the video, you also saw the tool used a third way—to make sense of a procedure. The teacher prompted the students to explain the long division algorithm using place value language. The tool—in this case, base ten blocks—supported the students in developing a conceptual understanding of the algorithm. As shown in this video, students can better visualize mathematical relationships with the assistance of manipulatives and other concrete models (NCTM, 2014).

Teachers can support conceptual understanding developed through the use of manipulatives with a concrete-representational-abstract (CRA) instructional sequence (Butler, Miller, Crehan, Babbitt, & Pierce, 2003). In a CRA instructional sequence, teachers first introduce students to a new concept with *concrete* tools, such as manipulatives. During the next part of the learning progression, instruction includes *representations* of the concept, such as drawings or other tools. In the final part of the learning progression or sequence, teachers illustrate the concept with *abstract* symbols, such as numerals. The key is that these stages must all be connected. All too often, due to time constraints or an oversight, teachers skip the representational step. Teachers provide students with concrete experiences using manipulatives and then introduce students to the abstract algorithms or procedures without connection. In their study

"Fraction Instruction for Students With Mathematics Disabilities: Comparing Two Teaching Sequences," researchers Frances M. Butler, Susan P. Miller, Kevin Crehan, Beatrice Babbitt, and Thomas Pierce (2003) find that students who are provided with the representational connection between using manipulatives and learning procedures outperform those who do not have access to that step. Concrete materials, or tools, play a major role in supporting students in developing a deeper understanding of mathematical concepts as long as the tools are connected to the procedures they support.

For example, you viewed the video about three-digit addition and watched as students used the base ten blocks to make sense of the problem. The base ten blocks provide the students with the opportunity to make a connection using concrete and tangible materials. A representation would be drawings of base ten blocks in place of the blocks. Finally, students would apply strategies using only the numbers as representation of the concrete and representations for base ten. The importance of providing each of these experiences and linking them to one another cannot be underestimated. See figure 1.7 for an image of the CRA sequence for the process of learning how to solve 376 + 258.

Concrete	Representation			Abstract
	Hundreds	Tens	Ones	376
	□ □ □	IIIIIII	: :	+258
	□ □	IIIII	: : : : :	634

Figure 1.7: CRA sequence for solving a three-digit addition task.

Knowing the significance of tools in supporting students' conceptual development, think back to the grade 1 Compare Objects Using Indirect Measurement lesson (page 24). What tools were used in that lesson? What was the purpose of the tools? The teacher provided the students with various tools—tiles, straws, and several objects. The learning goal in this lesson was for students to be able to indirectly compare objects' lengths. The tiles served as the standard unit of measure. Once students measured the straw as being five tiles long, they could then use the straw to represent a length of five tiles. The teacher provided other objects to help students understand how they could make indirect comparisons between new objects and the straw to determine whether an object measured more or less than five tiles. In this situation, the tools served as a way to develop conceptual understanding of indirect comparison. Following is a list of different purposes tools serve.

- Tools support students in making sense of the task.
- Tools support students in finding solutions to the task.
- Tools support students in developing conceptual understanding.
- Tools support students in connecting concepts to procedures.
- Tools support students in sharing their thinking about the mathematics.

Throughout this book, you will see many different types of tools used in the videos. Our definition of tools in mathematics teaching and learning does not need to be limited to manipulatives. Visual models or drawings are also examples of tools that support student learning and problem solving. As you read the rest of this book and watch the videos of small-group instruction, ask yourself how tools support the students in solving problems and developing conceptual understanding.

Centers

During small-group instruction, a teacher focuses his or her attention on advancing the learning of an intentionally selected group of students. The teacher typically brings these students to a separate location, such as a small table, within the classroom. This often occurs while the rest of the students in the class work independently. The remaining students might also work in *centers*. Centers are areas in the classroom where the teacher has preplanned for students to work independently or in small groups, frequently on a topic similar to that of the pulled small group. For mathematics centers to be valuable, teachers need to ensure students in the centers have the opportunity to engage with the mathematics in a meaningful way. Some questions to help teachers select and develop meaningful centers are as follows.

- What is the mathematical learning goal of the center?
- In what ways is the mathematics in the center meaningful?
- Is the mathematics in the center appropriate for the grade level?
- How has the center been organized so that students can complete the mathematics in the center on their own while benefiting from collaborating with others?
- In what ways do students receive immediate corrective feedback in the center?
- What strategies are in place to hold students accountable for the work they complete in the center?

Too often, centers are developed and implemented for the sole purpose of keeping the rest of the class occupied so that the teacher can work with a small group of students. Because centers may take up a large portion of students' instructional time, it is imperative they provide meaningful learning opportunities for students. To ensure a center is meaningful, teachers must think about the purpose, or learning goal, of the center. Having a set purpose for the center will help guarantee that the instructional time contributes to students' overall understanding of the mathematics.

The question, In what ways do students receive immediate corrective feedback in the center? is essential for centers that focus on developing students' procedural skill and procedural fluency. A center that requires students to repeatedly practice a procedure without opportunities to check their work along the way is unlikely to be helpful. Assigning roles within a center encourages students to collaborate and learn from one another. In addition to assigning one student the role of group leader, you might assign one student the role of confirming the group's answer with a preset answer key. This will ensure that students receive immediate corrective feedback and have the opportunity to make necessary corrections to the procedures they use.

If the center does not lend itself to collaborative learning, another way to build in the opportunity for students to receive immediate feedback is through the use of a *self-check folder*. Including a folder with the answers to the center's procedural practice problems will allow students to monitor their own learning during the center rotation. If you use individual task cards in the center and have access to tablets in your classroom, you might also consider creating a QR code that will direct students to the correct answer. Place the QR code on the task card so that students may use it to check their answers after performing the indicated calculation.

Conclusion

In this chapter, we focused on the various aspects of best practices in effective small-group instruction. We discussed how small-group instruction can support students in developing conceptual understanding. We created a shared image of what effective small-group instruction looks like in action through classroom videos. But recognizing effective small-group instruction and having the ability to plan for small-group instruction are very different. How can you use what you have learned to help you plan for your own pulled small groups? The following list of questions will support you in considering the structure of effective small-group instruction. We encourage you to consider these questions with your teacher team so you are prepared to productively use pulled small groups during mathematics instruction.

- **Learning goal:** What mathematical understanding, or piece of knowledge, do you want students to take away from this lesson?

- **Grouping:** What type of grouping will support the learning goal? Are you asking students to develop conceptual understanding? Are you providing students opportunities for problem solving? Or is the focus on gaining proficiency with a procedure?

- **Tools:** What tool or tools will support students in making sense of the task, finding solutions to the task, and developing understanding?

- **Facilitation of learning:** How will you monitor student understanding, address common errors, and advance or scaffold student thinking? What behaviors will you expect students to exhibit?

The best practices explored in this chapter create a vision for how your small-group instruction might look. As you continue reading, you will see how these practices form the foundation for learning within the pulled small group. The next chapter will provide you with more information regarding planning for small-group instruction. How does the task you select impact student learning? What types of questions can you ask to help students reason about the mathematics? What evidence can you collect within your formative assessment process to determine whether students have achieved the learning goal? The next chapter will explore these questions through the frame of the TQE process: selecting tasks, using productive questions, and collecting evidence.

CHAPTER 2

The TQE Process in Small-Group Instruction

Teachers should determine their use of pulled small groups based on the students' needs to achieve a specific learning goal. Too often, teachers use small-group instruction merely because of the expectation that they use it in every lesson. We strongly caution against this practice. However, when its use is warranted, like with all classroom instruction, effective small-group instruction begins in the planning stage.

In this chapter, we present a model for planning and implementing small-group instruction: the TQE process. We discuss how this model can help teachers prepare tasks, utilize questions, and elicit evidence of student learning in small groups. We then present a planning tool to help teachers utilize the TQE process in their own classrooms.

The TQE Process

The TQE process, previously described in *Making Sense of Mathematics for Teaching Grades K–2* (Dixon, Nolan, Adams, Brooks, & Howse, 2016) and *Making Sense of Mathematics for Teaching Grades 3–5* (Dixon, Nolan, Adams, Tobias, & Barmoha, 2016), is a framework for planning and enacting whole-class and small-group instruction. It provides a structure for selecting *tasks* to address specific learning goals, using productive *questions* to engage students in the Mathematical Practices, and collecting *evidence* of student understanding (or lack of understanding) to determine whether students have met the learning goals (see figure 2.1). This process is fluid and interrelated; teachers can use evidence to influence tasks and questions, ask questions to elicit evidence and determine the necessity of new tasks, and create tasks that lead to questions and evidence of student understanding.

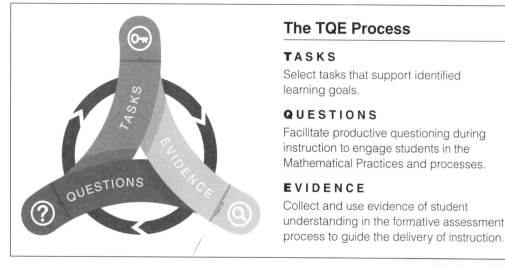

The TQE Process

TASKS

Select tasks that support identified learning goals.

QUESTIONS

Facilitate productive questioning during instruction to engage students in the Mathematical Practices and processes.

EVIDENCE

Collect and use evidence of student understanding in the formative assessment process to guide the delivery of instruction.

Source: Dixon, Nolan, & Adams, 2016, p. 4.

Figure 2.1: The TQE process.

What does the TQE process look like during small-group instruction? How do teachers support tasks during small-group instruction so that they ensure the tasks address the learning goal? To answer these questions, please consider the task in figure 2.2. Take a moment to solve this problem before you continue reading.

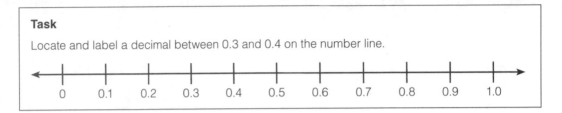

Task

Locate and label a decimal between 0.3 and 0.4 on the number line.

Figure 2.2: Focus task for the video lesson Locate and Name Decimals on a Number Line to the Hundredths Place.

Now, watch the video of a grade 4 small-group lesson Locate and Name Decimals on a Number Line to the Hundredths Place featuring students solving the same task. Notice how the teacher facilitates instruction through the use of a carefully selected task that addresses the learning goal. The learning goal in this video is for students to locate decimals to the hundredths place on a number line diagram, a goal that this lesson supports. Consider the following guiding questions in figure 2.3 related to the TQE process as you watch the video, and record your observations. These guiding questions are meant simply to get you started thinking about using the TQE process; we will discuss the individual elements in detail later in this chapter.

Locate and Name Decimals on a Number
Line to the Hundredths Place:

SolutionTree.com/GR4DecimalHundredths

Tasks
- How does the focus task connect to the learning goal?
- How does the teacher determine whether students are ready for the focus task?

Questions
- How does the teacher use questions to engage students with the Mathematical Practices?
- How does the teacher use questions to uncover potential common errors?

Evidence
- What evidence does the teacher collect of how students are or are not meeting the learning goal?

Figure 2.3: Guiding questions for observing the TQE process during small-group instruction.

It is helpful to determine students' positions along the learning progression prior to introducing the task for the learning goal. You may be able to make this determination from the use of the formative assessment process during whole-group instruction, or you may need to use the time in small-group instruction to obtain a clearer picture of individual students' understandings. For example, this small-group activity begins with two tasks that address prerequisites to the learning goal for the small-group lesson. In this case, the teacher needs to determine whether the students can estimate the placement of tenths on an open number line by using the benchmarks 0, 0.5, and 1. She also wants to see whether the students can work with decimals greater than 1.

The students are asked to locate 0.7 on a number line diagram. The teacher does not provide them with the number line diagram but expects them to create one on their whiteboards. She stops the group when she sees Joseph, the student in the orange T-shirt, placing the seventh hash mark at less than half the distance between 0 and 1. Even though he seems to notice his error and begins correcting his work, the teacher uses the evidence of the error as a basis for asking questions regarding how to determine the location of 0.7 on the number line.

Stopping student work here and facilitating the small group to discuss the error allows the teacher to engage the students in Mathematical Practice 3, "Construct viable arguments and critique the reasoning of others." Her questions focus the students' attention on critiquing one another's reasoning regarding how to determine the placement of 0.7. The teacher collects sufficient evidence to determine that it is not necessary for all the students to complete this preliminary task because students have met this prerequisite to the learning goal.

This illustrates that teaching students in a pulled-small-group setting affords the teacher a close-up look at students' understandings, which may negate the need to support tasks to their completion. This time-saving strategy is often not possible in whole-class instruction because it is difficult to know whether each and every student has met the targeted learning goal for a specific task. Although the implementation of this strategy is more reasonable in small-group instruction, teachers rarely use it. Have you used it or witnessed its use? How comfortable would you be if you moved on to another task before facilitating students to complete the task at hand? This is a good discussion topic for a collaborative team, as it helps respond to the frequent lament, "There's just not enough time!"

The second prerequisite task calls for the students to locate and name a decimal between 1.7 and 1.9. Again, the teacher does not provide the number line. The teacher looks for evidence that the students can order decimals and represent them on a number line diagram and that they can estimate the location of a decimal between 1.7 and 1.9. The students successfully locate 1.8 on the number line; however, the students do not all do so in the same way. The choice of asking students to draw the number line themselves, rather than plot the numbers on a provided prelabeled number line, provides the opportunity for the various representations. Sometimes, the tools teachers don't provide are just as important as the ones they do.

By prompting the students to look at one another's number lines and think about what's the same and what's different, the teacher uses the evidence inherent in the students' work as an opportunity for them to make sense of one another's thinking. The teacher also begins to focus on the structure of decimals and supports the students as they engage in Mathematical Practice 7, "Look for and make use of structure."

Once the students demonstrate that they can describe the structure inherent in placing decimals to the tenths place on an open number line, the teacher decides they are ready for the focus task (see figure 2.2, page 32). Again, the teacher's questions support the students to engage in Mathematical Practice 7, but now the structure has to do with making sense of hundredths using the base ten, ten-to-one relationship. Specifically, the students need to understand the equivalence relationship of 3 tenths and 30 hundredths. She provides a number line this time, but it is marked with tenths even though the students will need to mark and label hundredths to complete the task. Again, the tool the teacher provides and the information it does and does not include are both important in reaching the learning goal. Notice how the setup of the task and the teacher's questions direct the students' attention to the structure of decimals and the base ten place value system.

The teacher allows the students time to process and work on the task. She stops them when she sees that they are struggling. Rather than providing scaffolding by modeling how to solve the task at this point, the teacher asks the students questions with the purpose of supporting them to explain their thinking. She does not provide judgment or support because her goal is to collect evidence of the students' understanding and common errors, as well as to let them make sense of each other's thinking. The students determine the solution to the task by examining one another's thinking. This results in the students gaining a much deeper understanding of decimals to the hundredths place than they would have if the teacher had modeled the solution for them. Ultimately, the teacher collects evidence of the students' thinking and is able to determine that the students have met the learning goal.

Now that you have seen the TQE process illustrated in a small-group setting, let's break down the process so you can replicate it in your classroom. The following sections will discuss how the use of tasks, questions, and evidence support learning during small-group instruction.

Tasks

Pulled small groups can serve many purposes; however, a learning goal should always drive those purposes. The learning goal, and students' trajectories for meeting that goal, should determine the need for small-group instruction. Once a teacher has determined that small-group instruction is appropriate, he or she needs to plan students' activity in that small group. We strongly encourage you to use the TQE process to support that planning. After making sense of the learning goal, the first step in planning with the TQE process is identifying a good task aligned to that learning goal.

When selecting a task it will be helpful to ask yourself, "What task will allow my students to engage with the learning goal?" Many teachers pay little attention to the actual task, preferring to use small-group instruction simply as an opportunity to practice solving routine computations with a preselected strategy or procedure. However, research indicates that the teacher's role of selecting tasks and using questions to engage students with the tasks is more important than acknowledging whether students' approaches to solving predictable tasks are correct (Stein, Engle, Smith, & Hughes, 2008). Tasks that ask students to perform a memorized routine limit the opportunities for students to think conceptually and make the appropriate mathematical connections, compared to tasks that create opportunities for students to think (Smith & Stein, 2011). So, how can teachers plan and implement tasks that encourage critical thinking and problem solving?

University of Pittsburgh professors of education Margaret S. Smith and Mary Kay Stein (2011) suggest five practices that teachers may adopt to facilitate productive mathematical discussions around challenging tasks. These practices are:

1. Anticipating students' responses to tasks

2. Monitoring students' responses as they work on the tasks

3. Selecting particular students to present their mathematical responses

4. Purposefully sequencing students' responses to be displayed for the whole class

5. Helping students make the mathematical connections between and among their peers' responses

Smith and Stein's (2011) process can also help teachers carefully plan tasks. The first practice of *anticipating students' responses* is important to do during the planning stage. We present a planning tool that will support you in this step later in the chapter (page 45). Once you and your collaborative team have identified possible student responses and solution strategies, *monitoring students' responses as they work on the tasks* refers to observing your students closely to get a clear image of their current understandings. In order to move each student's thinking forward, *select particular students* within the group to share their thinking. The *order* in which you ask students to share their thinking and solution strategies can help guide your conversation and lead students to achieving the learning goal. Finally, providing opportunities for students to *connect their own strategies and thinking to their classmates'* will deepen their understanding of the mathematical concepts. This is done through facilitating productive discourse during the small-group instruction and will be discussed in greater detail in the next chapter (page 49). Using these five steps, teachers can anticipate students' possible responses and make informed instructional decisions based on knowledge of students' current mathematical thinking.

Good tasks should allow each and every student to engage in sense making. This means that a good task should be challenging, engaging, and enlightening for students with varying levels of understanding. As discussed in chapter 1 (page 7), using tasks with multiple access points and solution methods is an effective way to meet the needs of students with different levels of understanding. Good tasks provide opportunities for students to engage in the Mathematical Practices and for teachers to uncover common errors in student thinking. Tasks such as these are often described as having *high cognitive demand* (Smith & Stein, 2012). Depending on where students are in their learning progression, teachers might select a high- or low-cognitive-demand task to be the focus of the small-group instruction. High-cognitive-demand tasks "require students to think conceptually" (Stein & Smith, 1998, p. 269) and help them make connections among mathematical concepts. Tasks with low cognitive demand offer opportunities for students to practice procedures that they have learned. Having a conversation around the task selected for small-group instruction and how it aligns with the lesson's learning goal gives administrators and collaborative teams a great way to create a shared purpose for the time spent in small-group instruction.

During task implementation, it is the teacher's job to constantly gauge students' understanding of the mathematics. Based on how students explain their thinking, the teacher should ask questions to address common errors and move student thinking forward. It is the teacher's role to provide just-in-time scaffolding. When implementing a high-cognitive-demand task, it is easy to accidentally lower the cognitive demand with the questions you choose to ask. Think back to the small-group lesson, Locate and Name

Decimals on a Number Line to the Hundredths Place (page 32). The task was challenging to the students in that it required them to connect their understanding of tenths to make sense of hundredths. How might the demand of the task been altered if the teacher had asked the students, "What happens when you place ten hash marks between three-tenths and four-tenths on the number line? What could we call each of those marks?" While these questions would likely have helped the students to solve the task more quickly, the necessity to reason and problem solve would have been lessened, thus lowering the cognitive demand of the task. Rewatch the video (see also figure 2.3, page 32) and compare the questions provided here with the types of questions the teacher actually asked. Keeping in mind the purpose of your questions and the impact they have on student thinking will help maintain the intended cognitive demand of the task throughout the lesson.

Creating good tasks can be challenging. However, it is often possible to adapt existing tasks to make them more worthwhile. You can increase a task's cognitive demand by focusing students' attention on solution *processes*, rather than just solutions. For example, you could ask students to explain and justify their answers, you could direct students to compare student work samples, or you could reduce the level of scaffolding embedded in the task. Another helpful strategy is to embed tasks in real-world contexts. Chapter 1 of *Beyond the Common Core: A Handbook for Mathematics in a PLC at Work®, Grades K–5* (Dixon, Adams, & Nolan, 2015) provides an excellent discussion on selecting, adapting, or creating appropriate tasks (see the following list for some ideas).

- Rather than providing a context, ask students to write a word problem for a given expression.

- Have students determine an expression to represent a situation.

- Require students to provide justifications for their solutions.

- Challenge students to solve problems using more than one solution method or representation.

- Have students make sense of provided solution strategies by completing the solution or justifying the steps.

- Make the task open ended so that multiple responses will satisfy the task.

- Transform a single-step problem to a multistep problem.

- Include the use of multiple representations in a task.

How often do you look for ways to *increase* the demand of a task? This may seem counterintuitive. After all, aren't you trying to help students solve problems more easily? Actually, you should look for opportunities for students to engage in a productive struggle so that they become resilient problem solvers. Resilient problem solvers are those who continue to engage in a sense-making activity even when their first attempts at solving a problem are not successful. Teachers should emphasize facilitating these experiences during whole-class instruction, but also during instruction in the small group.

Consider this task: *Brandon shared four cookies equally between himself and his four friends. How much of a cookie should each person get?* The task itself is not difficult to solve, even for students in grade 5. Students could simply draw four circles and then partition each circle into five equal parts. Apart from the challenge of drawing fifths of a circle, this task contains little to engage students. So how could the cognitive demand be increased?

Consider how changing the constraints of the task could provide students with more opportunities to engage in sense making. A well-constructed task allows the teacher to determine whether students lack necessary understanding of the learning goal. Consider the following cookie-sharing task, also involving four cookies being shared among five friends (figure 2.4).

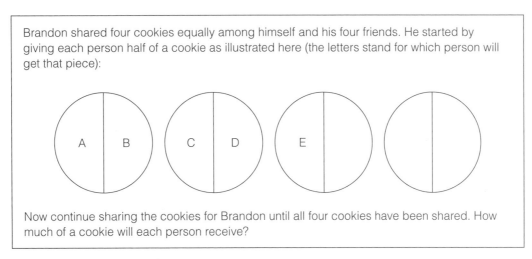

Source: Dixon, Nolan, Adams, Tobias, & Barmoha, 2016, p. 73.

Figure 2.4: Cookie-sharing task.

Note how the task increases the cognitive demand required of students by preventing them from simply dividing each cookie into five pieces. What type of thinking would students have to engage in to solve this task? Figure 2.5 provides an example of what a student might draw to solve the task.

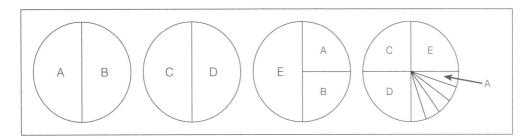

Source: Dixon, Nolan, Adams, Tobias, & Barmoha, 2016, p. 73.

Figure 2.5: Cookie-sharing task solution.

After drawing out the portions as illustrated in figure 2.5, the next step would be to name the pieces of cookie that Person A would receive. It is clear that Person A would receive ½ of the first cookie. The other cookie parts are often more challenging for students to name. What common errors might be elicited from students as they work to name the other cookie pieces? What common error would a student be making if the student named the next largest piece Person A would receive as ⅓? What about if the student named the smallest piece Person A would receive as ⅕? These common errors are intentionally inherent in the task. It may be new to you to consider a problem worthwhile because it has the potential to elicit common errors. However, it makes sense when you consider that you would prefer to address those errors during small-group instruction, rather than to see them on a summative assessment.

In the next video, the teacher begins with the simplistic cookie-sharing task to gauge where students are in the learning progression, but then she adapts the task to the one in figure 2.4 to increase the cognitive demand. The learning goal is for students to make sense of naming fractions to solve a problem involving adding fractions with unlike denominators. The original task would address exploring fractions as division, but it would not address the learning goal, nor would it have sufficient cognitive demand for use in a small group focused on developing conceptual understanding.

As you watch the video of the grade 5 small-group lesson Name Fractions With Unlike Denominators, notice how the teacher introduces the revised task. She is careful to minimize the just-in-case scaffolding she provides. She focuses on the students doing the sense making of the intended learning goal, rather than having them listen to her do the sense making. Common errors are more likely to surface when the students are able to share before the teacher explains. If the teacher were to unpack the problem for them, they would not have the opportunity to share their thinking and their errors might go unnoticed. This results in the teacher having the opportunity to address those errors and support students in deepening their understanding. Use the questions provided in figure 2.6 to guide your viewing before reading further.

Name Fractions With Unlike Denominators:
SolutionTree.com/GR5UnlikeDenominators

- What is the learning goal of this task?
- What is the original task?
- How has the teacher altered the original task?
- How does the revised task ensure that instruction will address the learning goal?
- With which Mathematical Practices do the students engage while exploring the task?
- What common errors are uncovered during the small-group lesson?
- To what extent do the students meet or fail to meet the learning goal during this lesson?

Figure 2.6: Guiding questions for observing task implementation during small-group instruction.

Planning tasks with both the learning goal and the Mathematical Practices in mind is crucial in order to most productively use the time in a pulled small group. Sometimes using just one task can be more effective in reaching the learning goal than using several tasks. The revised task in this lesson provides opportunities for students to engage in Mathematical Practice 1, "Make sense of problems and persevere in solving them," and Mathematical Practice 7, "Look for and make use of structure."

Notice how the teacher in this small-group video is careful to provide a task that requires perseverance to solve. She actually adjusts the task to increase the cognitive demand involved in solving it. The task is for Brandon to share four cookies among himself and four friends. Adding the constraint that each person needs to be given the largest possible unbroken piece before Brandon fairly shares the rest of the cookies increases the rigor of the task. The purpose of this modification is to ensure that students begin with pieces of cookie that are different sizes. The teacher wants students to begin with this representation because it increases the task's cognitive demand, but also because the learning goal is for students to make sense of adding fractions with unlike denominators. Before the teacher modifies the task, you see in the video how one student describes dividing each cookie into five pieces and giving four pieces to each person. This would give the students no need to find common denominators. This solution process would not engage students in meeting the learning goal with respect to content or practices. The modification ensures both.

The students struggle early on in solving this problem. They cannot see how to give each of the five people ½ of a cookie to start. They find ½ of each of the four cookies but neglect to see that when ½ is given, there is still another ½ of each cookie left to share. The teacher uses a helpful scaffolding strategy that also serves to develop the students' perseverance, rather than telling the students how to solve the problem. The teacher says, "Someone in the last group said that it worked. What could they have been saying?" This question renews the students' efforts to solve the task. They likely feel that if another student could determine the solution, then they should be able to do so as well.

The students determine how to give each of the five people ½ of a cookie, justify their solutions, and then fairly share the rest of the cookies. When the teacher asks the students, "What would Person A get altogether?" she is leading the students to represent the parts of the cookies as fractions with unlike denominators so they get at the learning goal of adding fractions with unlike denominators. She is also looking for evidence of the common error that the fractional part is determined by counting the number of pieces in the whole regardless of their relative sizes. Although ¼ of the cookie was originally named correctly as the second part of cookie that Person A gets, the teacher wants to collect evidence that all students understand why that part is ¼ and not ⅓. When she questions the students, they do provide evidence of a common error when they name this section ⅓. By anticipating this error, the teacher is able to facilitate deeper thinking around naming fractional parts. The makeup of the heterogeneous group aids her in addressing the error, as Desiree, the student in the blue shirt, is able to make sense of the error and help her classmates correctly name the fraction. This shows how heterogeneous groups are well suited for eliciting and resolving common errors.

The modified task provides an additional opportunity to address this persistent naming error when the teacher asks the students to name the smallest piece that each person will get. The error lingers, and interestingly, Desiree, who helped her classmates earlier, is the student who makes the error when naming ¹⁄₂₀. She names the piece ⅛ because she has cut her cookie into eight pieces, although the pieces are unequal. This time, Jonathan, the student in the gray shirt, helps *her* make sense of the proper name for this fraction. And this helps the teacher collect evidence that students will need more opportunities to solidify the learning goal. She makes the instructional decision to stop the task here, rather than have students combine the fractions with unlike denominators. While the students have not met the learning goal, they have worked through important prerequisites for meeting the learning goal. The modified task provided the opportunity for students to engage in the Mathematical Practices necessary to do the sense making.

The questions the teacher asked during task implementation were crucial for supporting this engagement and for collecting evidence of students' attainment, or lack of attainment, of the learning goal. The following section will discuss the qualities of effective questioning in small-group instruction.

Questions

As discussed in chapter 1 (page 7), the use of questioning can be a beneficial scaffolding technique. A tendency teachers must counteract when implementing tasks during small-group instruction is they often provide scaffolding too early. According to Margaret Walshaw and Glenda Anthony (2008), codirectors of the Centre for Research in Mathematics Education, teachers need to use scaffolding intentionally so that the scaffolding doesn't replace student thinking. Walshaw and Anthony (2008) go on to say that teachers must listen carefully to student responses so that teachers can contribute to discussions in supportive ways. They can do this through the use of questioning, re-voicing, and eliciting questions from other students.

Teachers can also use questions to prompt students to provide explanations and justifications, to engage students in specific Mathematical Practices, to elicit common errors, and to collect evidence that they have met the learning goal. Such questions make up the Q of the TQE process. The following is a list of general questions that are useful during small-group instruction.

- What did she or he say?
- Why does that work?
- How do you know?
- What is the same and what is different between your group members' solution strategies?
- What could you do next?
- How else could you solve it?
- What is a reasonable estimate?
- Are you sure?
- Do you agree?
- What did you do?

In the following video, the teacher chooses to extend the learning experience of the fourth-grade pulled small group discussed earlier in this chapter. The students were successful in locating a decimal between 0.3 and 0.4. Most students were able to make sense of hundredths. Consequently, the teacher uses the opportunity in the pulled small group to extend students' understanding of decimals to include thousandths with the lesson Locate and Name Decimals on a Number Line to the Thousandths Place. Use the questions provided in figure 2.7 to guide your viewing.

Locate and Name Decimals on a Number
Line to the Thousandths Place:

SolutionTree.com/GR4DecimalThousandths

- How does the teacher use questioning to provide just-in-time scaffolding as students work on the task?
- How does the teacher use questioning to engage students in the Mathematical Practices?
- How does the teacher use questioning to elicit a common error?
- In what ways does the teacher use questioning to facilitate students to make sense of one another's thinking?
- How does the use of questioning support students to meet the learning goal during this lesson?

Figure 2.7: Guiding questions for observing the use of questioning during small-group instruction.

The focus task for this small-group lesson represents an enrichment task (see figure 2.8). The content limit for this grade is to focus on decimals to the hundredths place. This enrichment task requires students to make sense of thousandths. The teacher chooses this task because the students demonstrated a deep understanding of the grade-level standard and she wants to take this opportunity to explore the same content but at a deeper level.

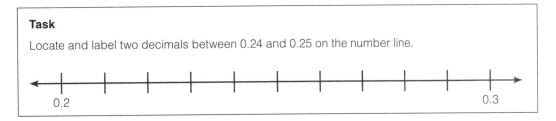

Task

Locate and label two decimals between 0.24 and 0.25 on the number line.

Figure 2.8: Focus task for the video lesson Locate and Name Decimals on a Number Line to the Thousandths Place.

The task is challenging. The teacher does not model the solution for the task because her goal is for the students to do the sense making. It would not serve the students well if the teacher used gradual release of responsibility, often referred to as "I do, we do, you do," which we described in the introduction (page 1). If she modeled the solution first, she would miss an opportunity to learn about the students' thinking. Instead, the teacher observes the students as they work on the task. She purposefully decides to have students work independently at first, as she wants to see how the students individually make sense of the task. She is looking for evidence of a specific error related to locating decimals on a number line diagram. First, she observes students as they work to see whether they correctly locate 0.24 and 0.25 on the open number line. She stops the students once she sees that Joseph, the student in the orange T-shirt, has made an error by locating these decimals between 0.2 and 0.21. The teacher asks the students a question—providing just-in-time scaffolding—so that they can uncover the error and correct it on their own. She asks them, "What's the same and what's different?" This simple question facilitates students to engage in Mathematical Practice 3, "Construct viable arguments and critique the reasoning of others." Cesar, the student in the striped shirt, does not agree with Joseph's placement of 0.24. Cesar is able to justify his position by using his understanding of decimals from the earlier pulled-small-group experience (see the grade 4 video Locate and Name Decimals on a Number Line to the Hundredths Place, shared on page 32). The teacher asks Joseph to reiterate what Cesar has shared to determine whether Joseph can now make sense of his error. Joseph's response provides evidence that he has made sense of his error, so the teacher returns the students to their individual efforts to solve the task without providing additional scaffolding.

When the students struggle to determine how to name thousandths, the teacher's questions turn to helping students find patterns in how decimals are named. She asks the students what she would have to do to find hundredths with a whole divided into tenths. Relying on her mathematics knowledge for teaching, she strategically decides to use tools to move from a number line diagram to a decimal square. She does this because she observes the students struggling to apply the pattern to partition length. She recognizes that switching to a different representation—an area model—supports students in determining the pattern. To push the students' thinking, she asks them to extend their understanding of the relationship between tenths and hundredths to determine the next decimal place. The students make sense of the task by responding to the teacher's questions and engaging in Mathematical Practice 8, "Look for and express regularity in repeated reasoning." The teacher uses questions to collect evidence that the students have made sense of thousandths using decimals.

Not only can questions serve as scaffolding of student learning, but targeted questions are also a helpful technique for collecting useful evidence of student learning. The following section will discuss the final step in the TQE process: gathering and making use of *evidence* to enhance student learning.

Evidence

By providing rigorous tasks and using questions that engage learners in the Mathematical Practices, teachers are able to collect evidence of students' understanding of the learning goal during small-group instruction. To gather evidence of student learning, the teacher will best use small-group time if he or she knows the common errors to look for during instruction. In this way, the teacher can make sure to ask questions that will elicit those common errors if they exist with students. The teacher can look for both evidence of common errors and evidence that students have met the learning goal during small-group instruction and subsequently use this evidence within a formative assessment process. When used appropriately in a formative assessment process, the evidence guides both task implementation and questioning and serves as part of a cyclical process in planning future learning opportunities.

Preparing opportunities to collect this evidence should occur prior to pulling the small group. However, as important as evidence is in guiding instruction, according to Dylan Wiliam (2018), teachers "rarely plan in detail how they are going to find out where the students are in their learning" (p. 83). For this reason, the TQE process requires that teachers make these needed preparations; it incorporates planning to collect evidence of student understanding and preparing tasks and questions. The following list provides examples of sources of evidence that can inform the TQE process.

- Verbal contributions during student-to-student discussions
- Verbal responses to questions posed by the teacher
- Written responses to tasks
- Drawings used to solve tasks
- Ways students use manipulatives
- Questions students ask the teacher and each other
- Students' facial expressions

Consider the following grade 1 video lesson, Relate Number of Partitioned Pieces to Size of Pieces. The teacher enters the small-group instruction with her learning goal in mind. Notice how the teacher adjusts her lesson based on what she learns about students' thinking through the evidence she collects. Use the questions provided in figure 2.9 to guide your viewing before reading further.

Relate Number of Partitioned Pieces to Size of Pieces:
SolutionTree.com/GR1PartitionedPieces

- What is the learning goal of this lesson?
- What tasks does the teacher use to support students to meet the learning goal?
- What evidence does the teacher seek to determine whether students have met the learning goal?
- What evidence do students provide that they are engaging in the Mathematical Practices?
- How does the teacher alter her questioning based on the evidence she collects?

Figure 2.9: Guiding questions for observing the collection of evidence during small-group instruction.

A benefit of small-group instruction is the ability to adapt instruction to meet the group's needs based on specific students' responses. In this setting, the small-group lesson serves as part of the ongoing formative assessment process. This lesson's learning goal is for the students to be able to reason about the size of fractions by demonstrating they understand that the more pieces a whole is partitioned into, the smaller the pieces in that whole. Here, you see the teacher asking an opening formative assessment question to determine the students' prior knowledge on fraction size. She shows a circle to represent a cookie and asks the students whether they would rather share the cookie with one other person or three other people. The evidence the students provide in the form of their responses surprises the teacher. The students respond that they would rather share with three other people. Instead of assuming the students do not understand the size of fractions based on how the whole is partitioned, the teacher uses questions (the second component of the TQE process) to gather additional evidence related to students' understanding of the learning goal. She asks the students, "Why?" Cola, the student in the white shirt, states that sharing with more people is "kind." The students' responses provide the teacher with the necessary evidence to tailor her instruction to their needs so she can help them meet the learning goal. She adjusts how she presents the task and asks, "What if you were trying to get the most amount of cookie possible? Would you want to share it with one other person or with three other people?" Two of the students answer that they would rather share with one other person, whereas the other two say they would rather share with three other people. This is the evidence the teacher seeks. She now knows that she needs to dive in deeper with this content by exploring related tasks and using questions to engage students in the Mathematical Practices.

Because the students in the group provide evidence of different levels of understanding of fraction size, the teacher realizes she needs to build this foundational understanding and make the concept more visual. She has prepared for this possibility by having cutout circles to represent cookies available for student use. She adapts her instruction and asks the students to draw on their cookie to show how they would share with one person. Alex, the student in the dark green T-shirt, splits his cookie in half, whereas the others split their cookie in fourths. Rather than assigning the solutions with the label *correct* or *incorrect*, the teacher uses the differences in the drawings to further student learning. She asks students to explain the differences between the cookie split in two and the cookie split in four. She is focusing students' attention on Mathematical Practice 7, "Look for and make use of structure."

Daylanie, the student in the light green T-shirt, expresses that when sharing the cookie split in two, each person would receive half the cookie. She displays an understanding of equivalence when expressing that each student would receive two pieces of the cookie that is split in four. However, she struggles with naming the unit fraction and incorrectly says that each person would receive two halves, rather than the correct answer of two fourths. Daylanie provides evidence that her understanding of naming fractions is tenuous at best.

Small-group instruction provides a good setting to reinforce the correct use of academic vocabulary and encourage students to engage in Mathematical Practice 6, "Attend to precision," because the teacher is able to hear and interpret the contributions of each and every participant in the group. The teacher asks probing questions until one student is able to identify each piece of the cookie split in four pieces as a quarter.

Returning to her learning goal, the teacher continues with the sharing cookies context. She asks the students what would happen if they shared a cookie among four people and then six people. Once the students respond that they would divide the cookie into four and six pieces, the teacher uses fraction circles to show a cookie split into fourths and one split into sixths. She asks the students to compare the size of each fractional part. The students are able to identify that the cookie divided into sixths results in smaller pieces. The teacher asks students to engage in Mathematical Practice 8, "Look for and express regularity in repeated reasoning," by inquiring about a cookie broken into twelve pieces. She then extends this understanding with a cookie broken into twenty pieces. The teacher intentionally selects a fraction that cannot be represented by fraction circles so she can collect evidence of the level of student understanding. At one point, Alex wants to share how the size of the fraction changes as the whole is divided into more pieces, but the teacher intentionally does not call on him, because she already knows he understands the concept. She would not gain any insight into the other students' levels of understanding by calling on Alex.

When providing small-group instruction using the TQE process, teachers have the capability of ensuring all students are processing the content through intentional questioning of each student. Not only can teachers make sure each student interacts with the content, but they can hold each student accountable for his or her own learning. Near the end of this video, the teacher chooses to call on Tanith, the student in the ruffle-sleeved top, who struggled in the beginning of the video. This student is able to make sense of the rule that the more pieces a whole is broken into, the smaller the pieces. This evidence shows the student has accomplished the learning goal.

Having discussed the TQE process in depth and provided examples of the process in action, we will now provide you with a lesson-planning tool aligned with this model that will assist you in planning with the TQE process and transferring it to your pulled small groups.

The TQE Process Lesson-Planning Tool

Teachers are more likely to incorporate rich tasks, productive questioning, and the use of evidence in the formative assessment process during small-group instruction if they plan these components of teaching in advance (Huinker & Bill, 2017; NCTM, 2014). The TQE process lesson-planning tool (see figure 2.10, pages 46–47) offers a structure for planning small-group instruction supportive of the teaching practices. Specifically, this tool first guides teachers to select tasks to meet a specified learning goal. Tasks may be taken directly from your published resource, adapted to more closely meet the learning goal, or be teacher-created. The tool also guides teachers to implement questions that support students to connect with tasks and to engage in the Mathematical Practices while eliciting common errors as necessary, and collect evidence of students' progress toward meeting the learning goal within a formative assessment process. A reasonable technique for beginning to use this tool is to identify an upcoming unit's three most important topics with your collaborative team. Then use the TQE process lesson-planning tool to plan for small-group instruction related to those three topics. The tool can be used in a similar fashion to plan for whole-class instruction based on the TQE process.

To guide you in using the TQE process lesson-planning tool, we provide two sample lesson plans that we created using the tool. Appendix A (page 71) provides a lesson plan for grades K–2, and Appendix B (page 73) depicts one for grades 3–5. We encourage you to use these as resources for beginning your own lesson plans using this template.

Conclusion

Now that you have read about the TQE process, consider how your current lesson planning and lesson implementation incorporate tasks, questions, and evidence. Where do you spend the most time? Does your collaborative team tend to linger on task selection during the planning process? How do you work together to craft questions that can be used during instruction? In what ways might you plan for the evidence you will collect for use in the formative assessment process? We encourage you to think about your current planning process and ways in which use of the TQE process could enhance student understanding. For example, your team may already carefully consider the tasks you will implement, and thus decide that you would like to spend more of your time focusing on the questions you will ask or the evidence you will collect.

TQE Process Lesson-Planning Tool

Learning Goal

What are your considerations for grouping students? Is it appropriate to use small-group instruction to meet this learning goal?

Task

This high-cognitive-demand task links to the learning goal and allows students to engage in the Mathematical Practices.

Record your task here:

What common errors might be elicited as students work on this task?

What tools will you use to support students to engage with the task?

What Mathematical Practices do you anticipate students engaging in as they work on this task?

Questions

These questions facilitate students to engage in the Mathematical Practices, elicit common errors and evidence of conceptual understanding, and offer scaffolding just in time.

Record your questions here:

Evidence	Record examples of evidence you will collect here:
This evidence is used to determine whether students have met the learning goal and to uncover common errors.	

Source: © 2017 by Juli K. Dixon, Edward C. Nolan, and Thomasenia Lott Adams.

Figure 2.10: TQE process lesson-planning tool.

Visit **go.SolutionTree.com/mathematics** for a free reproducible version of this figure.

While planning for small-group instruction is imperative, so is supporting students to engage in the lesson as you implement small-group instruction. What are your expectations for student interactions when pulling small groups? In the next chapter, we support you to investigate this question, as we turn our attention to supporting productive discourse during small-group instruction.

CHAPTER 3

Discourse in Small-Group Instruction

We have explored best practices in small-group instruction and discussed how to use the TQE process to plan for pulled-small-group time. However, you may still be wondering how to support the level of discourse observed in the videos you have watched thus far. In this chapter, we will answer the following questions: How do you support students to engage in productive discussions related to the learning goal? What are reasonable expectations for student contributions in small-group instruction? Let's begin this discussion by viewing an example of small-group discourse. We will then present five strategies for establishing effective discourse in the small group and discuss effective teaching practices that facilitate discourse.

Discourse During Small-Group Instruction

Before reading further, watch the small-group video of kindergarten students engaging in the lesson Count and Compare Cubes. Use the questions provided in figure 3.1 to guide your thinking.

Count and Compare Cubes:
SolutionTree.com/GRKCompareCubes

- What do you notice about how the teacher facilitates discussion?
- How are the students engaged in discussion?
- How does discourse support student learning in this lesson?

Figure 3.1: Guiding questions for observing discourse during small-group instruction.

In this video, the teacher challenges kindergarten students to make sense of number comparisons using cubes. Many students at this age are still learning number names, the counting sequence, and one-to-one correspondence. Comparisons can be difficult, but they provide a context to apply and build on these skills. By working with a peer within the small group, the students get the opportunity to have conversations as they make sense of this challenging concept.

Initially, the teacher asks the students to compare their cubes with their partner's cubes. The color of the cubes is purposefully used to distinguish between the two sets, and you see that Jayden and Daniel, the students with the red cubes, determine without prompting from the teacher that they have the same number of cubes. The open dialogue allows the students to construct natural and authentic connections to making a comparison as they realize that they both have sixteen cubes.

You see Neveiah, the student in the white shirt, struggle with the counting process. She is still building foundational counting skills and needs a little more time. Eventually, she is able to determine that she has fourteen cubes, and Jayden, her partner, states that he has more. The teacher asks Neveiah, "Are you sure he has more?" and "How do you know?"

Teachers can anticipate that students will occasionally try to talk over one another. The teacher asks Neveiah, who previously had difficulty counting her cubes, how she knows her partner has more cubes. Maybe you didn't even notice when Jayden jumps in to rescue her. He says, "Because I have sixteen and she has fourteen."

Rather than respond to Jayden, who spoke for Neveiah, the teacher asks Neveiah, "How do *you* know that he has more than you?" Notice that the teacher maintains the expectation that the student who is asked the question will answer. An important aspect of establishing rules for discourse is maintaining those rules over time. The practice of holding individual students accountable for their own part in the discussion helps establish the rules for discourse. This shows students that although their peers may try to take the lead, they are still individually responsible for their own explanations. Also, this practice allows the teacher to observe Neveiah's strategy and learn more about her thinking.

The teacher then asks the students to represent red having three more cubes than blue. This task is difficult because it is abstract for young learners. More challenging tasks like this provide opportunities for students to engage in meaningful discourse with one another. Also, this task has multiple solution strategies. Using tasks with multiple solution strategies is a way to increase the cognitive demand of tasks as well as the likelihood of productive discourse.

Neveiah, who struggled initially to count her cubes, struggles again and says that she has thirteen now, even though she did not remove any cubes from her collection. Rather than correct her, the teacher asks whether she is sure. It is important to ask students whether they are sure when they give a correct answer as well as when they give an incorrect one. This establishes the expectation that students should use reasoning to determine whether their answers are correct, rather than rely on the teacher to judge the accuracy of their work.

When Neveiah tries to pass the responsibility back to the teacher, the teacher uses it as an opportunity to reinforce her rule of student ownership of mathematical reasoning and to have the student practice the skill of counting. When she miscounts again, the teacher has her count out loud in hopes that she will count more carefully. This also gives everyone at the table the opportunity to observe her counting and to determine whether and where an error is made.

The teacher's questioning strategies orient the students to the task at hand. She also provides a hint that they do not need to use all their cubes. Rather than telling the students that they have not represented three more red than blue, she asks the students whether that is what they are showing. Upon considering this question, they are able to identify that they haven't figured out how to model the task's problem and that they are initially unsure how to show three more red than blue.

When the students determine a way to correctly represent the solution to the task, the teacher brings the group together and has the students explain. They must listen and watch carefully so they can decide whether they agree with the offered solution. As norms are established, it is important that students understand that it is okay to disagree and they should feel comfortable making mistakes and asking questions when necessary. Supporting students to evaluate their peers' reasoning helps them develop proficiency with Mathematical Practice 3, "Construct viable arguments and critique the reasoning of others." As they recheck their work and the work of their peers they engage in Mathematical Practice 6, "Attend to precision."

Meaningful Classroom Discourse

A focus on student discourse is a hallmark of best practice in mathematics education. Pioneering psychologist Lev Vygotsky (1934/1994) establishes the importance of students talking as they make sense of mathematics on a personal level. NCTM (1991) provides specific guidelines for highlighting meaningful mathematical discourse in the book *Professional Standards for Teaching Mathematics*. They provide six standards for teaching mathematics, of which two of those standards focus on specific roles in discourse. Standard 2 guides our thinking about the teacher's role in discourse and standard 3 focuses on the role of the students:

Standard 2: The Teacher's Role in Discourse

The teacher of mathematics should orchestrate discourse by—

- posing questions and tasks that elicit, engage, and challenge each student's thinking;
- listening carefully to students' ideas;
- asking students to clarify and justify their ideas orally and in writing;
- deciding what to pursue in depth from among the ideas that students bring up during a discussion;
- deciding when and how to attach mathematical notation and language to students' ideas;
- deciding when to provide information, when to clarify an issue, when to model, when to lead, and when to let a student struggle with a difficulty;
- motivating students' participation in discussions and deciding when and how to encourage each student to participate.

Standard 3: Students' Role in Discourse

The teacher of mathematics should promote classroom discourse in which students—

- listen to, respond to, and question the teacher and one another;
- use a variety of tools to reason, make connections, solve problems, and communicate;
- initiate problems and questions;
- make conjectures and present solutions;
- explore examples and counterexamples to investigate a conjecture;
- try to convince themselves and one another of the validity of particular representations, solutions, conjectures, and answers;
- rely on mathematical evidence and argument to determine validity. (NCTM, 1991, pp. 35, 45)

Too often, small-group instruction strays from these recommendations and instead focuses on providing step-by-step instruction and modeling procedures in hopes of filling gaps in student understanding.

Although teachers may implement these strategies with the best of intentions, their implementation sends the clear message that the ownership of ideas belongs to the teacher rather than the students. Instead, teachers and teaching strategies should aim to position the students as the active participants in constructing knowledge. The students should take ownership of their learning, and the teacher should orchestrate discussions.

Research on best practices in mathematics education suggests that students do not simply absorb information that the teacher provides. Rather, in order to learn and retain information successfully, they must experience opportunities to struggle with, discuss, and make personal connections to the mathematics (Carpenter, Fennema, Franke, Levi, & Empson, 2015). When students participate in meaningful discourse, they make sense of the mathematics as they engage with their peers. They work together as a small-group community to support one another. They also learn from one another and are able to share unique perspectives about the mathematics.

Effective Discourse in the Small Group

NCTM's (1991) teaching standards describe the teacher and student roles and responsibilities required to support the sort of discourse necessary for students to take ownership of their knowledge. But how do you facilitate students to take ownership of their learning in small-group instruction? This might be a useful topic of discussion within your collaborative team. Here, we present five strategies teachers can use to implement productive discourse in a small group.

1. Facilitating productive discourse patterns

2. Creating small-group norms

3. Establishing rules

4. Setting expectations

5. Supporting students to engage in discourse

Facilitating Productive Discourse Patterns

A *discourse pattern* can best be described as the ways the teacher and the students interact with one another in a classroom or small-group setting. A typical pattern of talk often seen during mathematics lessons is described as *initiation, response, evaluation* (IRE; Mehan, 1979). When this discourse pattern is in place, the teacher initiates talk by asking a low-complexity question. The teacher then selects a student to provide a response to the question. Then, the teacher evaluates the correctness of the student's response and shares that determination. This pattern establishes the teacher as the one who controls the conversation and the students as recipients of information whom the teacher occasionally allows into the conversation, often only when they can supply a correct answer.

Important changes take place when teachers replace this pattern with *initiation, demonstration, evaluation* or *elaboration* (IDE; Nathan, Eilam, & Kim, 2007). The IDE pattern begins with a question or problem that either the teacher or a student initiates. The next step occurs when students demonstrate their understanding. Rather than merely provide an answer, the student's contribution at this point should provide information and establish a shared meaning of the response with other students. Students then either evaluate their understanding and the understanding of their peers or elaborate on their own thoughts in response to their peers. This elaboration might take the form of additional explanation, adjustments to explanations, or clarifying questions. Table 3.1 provides a comparison of these two discourse patterns.

Table 3.1: IRE and IDE Discourse Patterns

IRE Pattern of Discourse	IDE Pattern of Discourse
The teacher *initiates* a question (often closed).	Either the teacher or a student *initiates* a question (often open ended) or problem.
Students *respond* to the teacher.	Students *demonstrate* their understanding with the expectation that it will be beneficial to other students.
The teacher *evaluates* the student's response.	Students *evaluate* their understanding and that of their peers. Students *elaborate* on their thoughts in response to their peers.

Source: Adapted from Brooks, 2014.

Note how the last step in an IRE pattern completes the exchange of information, whereas the last step in IDE encourages participants to share more information, which often leads them to ask and answer more questions. The features that distinguish IDE from IRE are best described as student-focused strategies, rather than the teacher-focused strategies seen with the IRE pattern of discourse. These discourse patterns can define interactions during small-group instruction. To illustrate, the IRE discourse pattern could be likened to a game of ping-pong. The teacher begins the conversation and serves the ping-pong ball over to one student. The student's response sends the ping-pong ball back to the teacher to check for correctness. It is now the teacher's turn to evaluate the response. In the IDE pattern of discourse, the game no longer looks like a traditional ping-pong game because there are more than two players. Instead, the interactions resemble a game of volleyball. Either a teacher or a student begins the conversation and sends the volleyball into the air among the small group. A classmate responds and sends the volleyball to whoever would like to evaluate or elaborate on the current thinking. Then, he or she tosses the ball into the air for another groupmate to grab. Anyone in the group is welcome to join the game and conversation. At times, a group might even have more than one volleyball as peers discuss their thoughts with partners within the small group.

It is the teacher's responsibility to establish the expectations for how students should interact with the content, the teacher, and one another in the small group, which is the focus of the next section. We will begin with an explanation of norms, rules, and explanations.

Creating Small-Group Norms

We define *norms* as established ways of behaving. As with other aspects of small-group instruction, teachers should carefully consider norms. They need to be planned, taught, and practiced. Your actions in the pulled small group should highlight and support the norms. Paying explicit attention to the establishment of effective norms is an important aspect of small-group instruction.

The teacher needs to intentionally establish these norms in the small-group setting. This is true regardless of whether these norms have been established for whole-class discussion, as one norm will not necessarily transfer to the other setting. Rather, you will need to establish norms for discourse for both whole-group and small-group settings.

You should not expect students to immediately understand your expectations. Rather, you will need to systematically establish the norms and support them over time (Dixon, Andreasen, & Stephan, 2009). Here, we provide a short list of norms appropriate for any mathematics classroom, discussed in *Making Sense of Mathematics for Teaching Grades K–2* (Dixon, Nolan, Adams, Brooks, & Howse, 2016) and *Making Sense of Mathematics for Teaching Grades 3–5* (Dixon, Nolan, Adams, Tobias, & Barmoha, 2016). You may choose to use these three norms or create your own.

1. Explain and justify solutions.

2. Make sense of each other's solutions.

3. Say when you don't understand or when you don't agree.

Some students, especially at the elementary level, may have difficulty adapting to norms. In these cases, establishing rules can be helpful in ensuring they understand how to engage in small-group mathematics lessons. For this reason, you may find it helpful to create norms and also establish classroom rules. Rules are established to help students understand and model the norms we hope to create.

Establishing Rules

Upon hearing these norms, some students may immediately grasp how to adhere to them during small-group instruction. Others will need additional support in understanding the actions and behaviors that the norms require. Explicit rules can provide this support for teachers and students in the establishment of norms.

The purpose of rules is to set expectations about student engagement in meaningful mathematics discussions. The rules should reflect your beliefs about student learning. We have found that it is sometimes helpful to provide specific rules to support young learners as they make sense of the expectations (Brooks & Dixon, 2013). By highlighting your specific rules about engaging in discussions, you can provide a framework of expected behavior for students. Their prior experiences with learning mathematics may differ greatly from this framework, so the more specific you can be, the better they will understand their new role in the process. These five rules support classrooms in establishing discourse norms for small-group instruction.

1. **Explain your thinking:** Students may be accustomed to giving answers, but often, they have less familiarity with explaining the thinking that led them to those answers. As students get more comfortable with this rule, they will automatically discuss their thought processes when they share answers.

2. **Listen when others are speaking:** This rule sets the expectation that students look at the speaker and think about what is being shared. Their goal is to make sense of what the other person shares.

3. **Say whether you agree or disagree:** This is a direct outcome of the second rule. As students are listening to one another, they should be critically analyzing the strategies and methods that their peers share. If they think someone has made a mistake, they are expected to disagree respectfully. Likewise, if they agree with what a student shares, they are to join the discussion by stating their agreement and possibly adding more to what was shared. Students need to learn that disagreements are allowable and that they can voice their thoughts in a way that is helpful to everyone in the group.

4. **Talk about what the speaker shared before sharing your own work:** We purposefully include this in the rules because students often focus on their own strategies, rather than on demonstrating they understand what another student has shared. This rule sets an expectation for a level of listening that goes beyond just hearing; instead, it causes students to respond in a meaningful way to the other students in the group. Once they connect to a shared strategy, they can add how their own strategy may be alike or different.

5. **Own and share your thinking:** It will be obvious that students are following this rule when they refuse to let other group members sway them until they are convinced on a personal level. This is the level of ownership you want from your students.

We will continue to examine these rules throughout the chapter and will look for them in action in the small-group videos. How can you establish these rules during small-group instruction? It is helpful to present the rules at the beginning of the school year. You should revisit them often, and students should participate in conversations about what each rule means. Young learners may need time to make sense of the rules. Students will benefit from your pointing out when they are following the rules as well as when they are deviating from them during mathematics lessons.

Expect that students will require reminders and redirection from time to time. You may also find it helpful to have conversations with students about how to use language. Students who struggle with finding words to convey their thinking might benefit from the use of sentence stems or frames. Consider providing students with a particular sentence frame or set of sentence frames that gives them a structure for engaging in the conversation. Figure 3.2 provides examples of sentence frames. You can adapt these to suit the needs of your students.

- I think the answer is _____ because _____.
- I wonder about _____ because _____.
- My solution strategy was like _____ because _____.
- My solution strategy was different from _____ because _____.
- I think you are right about _____, but I don't think you are right about _____.
- I agree with _____'s idea because _____.
- I disagree with _____'s idea because _____.
- I agree with your idea because _____.
- I disagree with your idea because _____.
- _____ thinks _____, but I think _____.
- I am confused about _____. Can you explain that again?
- I would like to add on to what _____ said. I also think _____.
- This reminds me of _____ because _____.

Figure 3.2: Sentence frames for helping students engage in meaningful discourse.

*Visit **go.SolutionTree.com/mathematics** for a free reproducible version of this table.*

In the following video of grade 3 students focused on area (page 56), think about how the teacher may have established the five rules with these young learners before they started their group work. Also consider how the teacher might work to further establish the rules with the students. Consider the questions in figure 3.3 (page 56) to guide you as you watch.

        Find Area and Order by Size:
SolutionTree.com/GR3AreaOrder

- What rules are in place regarding discourse during the lesson?
- How do students engage with one another during the lesson?
- What discourse norms are yet to be established?

Figure 3.3: Guiding questions for observing the rules for discourse in small-group instruction.

In this video, students work together to put shapes in order based on their areas. You may notice that some discourse norms are evident, while others are yet to be developed. The teacher plays an important role in guiding the students. She has the students discuss what they are doing as they start the task. As they share their processes, it becomes apparent that one student has confused area with perimeter. The teacher asks the other students what they think so that they can state whether they disagree. Mitchell, the student in the striped shirt, does just that and also explains that placing the squares along the outside would result in finding the perimeter and not the area.

When Grace, the student in the white shirt, comes up with a question about whether she should count the square she placed in one corner, she poses the question to the group. The students understand that the expectation is for them to respond. Joey, the student in the black shirt, nods his head yes. Mitchell, who doesn't understand, asks Grace what she means. It is interesting to see Grace respond to the teacher rather than to the student who asked what she means. This indicates that the students are not yet accustomed to speaking to one another. You see this again when the teacher says they should discuss her question with each other. Some students think that Grace does need to count the square in the corner twice, and some say that she does not, but rather than discussing it with each other, the students demonstrate that they have been conditioned to speak to the teacher rather than their peers. It is clear the students are accustomed to the typical IRE ping-pong game of discourse. You hear Allyana, the student in the denim vest, say, "She still has the middle part . . ." almost as if Grace is not there. The teacher later reinforces the rule of listening to others by reminding them of that expectation.

The establishment of expectations is critical when facilitating student conversations and responses to one another during small-group work. We will discuss ways to effectively set expectations in the following section.

Setting Expectations

You can set expectations for students both explicitly and implicitly through your interactions with students. It is important to be explicit about your expectations around discourse while also being mindful of what you communicate through your interactions. At times, it may be necessary to model expectations. For example, you may share a blatantly wrong answer and encourage students to help you by correcting the error. Students can benefit from this type of practice as they learn to be comfortable with their classmates disagreeing with them as well as with the expectation that they may disagree with their classmates.

An example of setting expectations implicitly is illustrated in how you respond to students when they share answers. If you are quick to correct students or to tell them when they are correct, they will think, through those interactions, that you value only correct answers. On the other hand, if you take the time to highlight student discourse and to question more than you tell, students will learn that you value their thinking as well. Consider the task in figure 3.4 as we explore setting expectations indirectly.

> **Task**
>
> Blake and Jordan each bought the same type of candy bar. Blake ate ¾ of his candy bar, and Jordan ate ⅚ of his. Who ate more of their candy bar?

Figure 3.4: Focus task for the video lesson Compare Fractions With a Linear Model.

As you watch the following video associated with this task, use the questions in figure 3.5 to guide your considerations regarding the expectations about discourse that are present in this grade 4 small-group lesson on fraction comparison.

Compare Fractions With a Linear Model:
SolutionTree.com/GR4CompareFractions

- What does the teacher communicate explicitly to the students about her role in the small group?
- What does the teacher communicate indirectly regarding the students' roles in the small group?
- How does the teacher reinforce her expectations regarding discourse during the lesson?
- How do the students respond to the expectations regarding discourse?

Figure 3.5: Guiding questions for observing expectations for discourse during small-group instruction.

As students engage in tasks related to fractions, manipulatives are especially important for developing connections to concepts (Butler et al., 2003). The tangible items not only connect students to the concepts but also provide a framework for explaining students' reasoning about fractions. There are three different ways to represent fractions with manipulatives or models. The three fraction models are set, length, and area. For more information, see *Making Sense of Mathematics for Teaching Grades 3–5* (Dixon, Nolan, Adams, Tobias, & Barmoha, 2016). Too often, fraction representations are only explored with an area model, such as with pizzas and pattern blocks. When teachers *only* use the area model, the conversation is limited since they miss important opportunities for students to have a thorough understanding of different representations for fractional amounts.

What you see in this fraction comparison lesson is the students using a *linear* model represented with Cuisenaire rods. The students are making sense of a word problem requiring them to represent a candy bar that can be modeled with both fourths and sixths. To set the stage for using the model, the teacher first asks the students to make observations about the rods.

The teacher orients the students to using the Cuisenaire rods to solve the word problem by asking them what they think they will do with the rods. Jose, the student in the green shirt, shares his thoughts about using the biggest one, the orange rod, to represent the whole candy bar. Although the orange rod is the longest, it cannot be used to represent the whole when the goal is to show ¾ or ⅚ using the other Cuisenaire rods. Rather than bringing this to his attention, the teacher deliberately engages the other students by asking them to critique his reasoning. By asking, "What do you think about what he just said?" she places the conversation and the expectation for sense making with the students. When Maggie, the student in the blue floral shirt, asks Jose to repeat what he said, it indicates that an established norm of listening to one another is evident to the students. Often, a first step of a critique is to have heard and understood what was shared. That is why it is important to establish listening as one of the discourse norms within the pulled small group and then to set the expectation to do so.

When asked to repeat his reasoning, Jose states that because the orange is taller than all the other rods, that means orange is the whole. Again, the teacher deliberately chooses not to correct Jose and instead allows him to explore that thought. This choice allows Jose to reach his own conclusion based on his work with the Cuisenaire rods. The teacher asks the other students what they think about Jose's strategy. Notice how the response that follows does not directly address the information that was just provided. Maggie begins to share her own strategy instead of commenting on the strategy that Jose shared. Rather than allowing Maggie to continue with her own strategy, the teacher redirects her to react to Jose's strategy. This is an explicit attempt to establish the expected norms for discourse within the small group. Students often need help developing these conversational skills. It is important to set the expectation that students first respond to what was shared before sharing their own strategies. This is a way to reinforce the norm of listening to one another.

The teacher highlights the importance of identifying the length of the whole candy bar, but then allows the students to make sense of the task either individually or with a partner. She introduces the model of the Cuisenaire rods arranged in order of length to help students make a connection to how each color relates to the others. This task is purposefully designed to help the students see the relationships among the different colored rods and then recognize the different fractional lengths that can be shown with the rods. By bringing the students' attention to how the lengths of the rods compare to one another, the teacher is supporting students with Mathematical Practice 7, "Look for and make use of structure." Through this the focus remains on students making sense of the representations, explaining their thinking, and paying attention to the explanations of others.

You should notice that the teacher allows the students to engage in productive struggle. By allowing the students to explore incorrect strategies, she helps them reach an understanding about how to represent the fractional amounts of ¾ and ⅚ of the same length whole. She provides time for students to struggle and practice perseverance so they can make personal connections, rather than the teacher explaining a solution strategy and doing the thinking for them. This requires students to engage in Mathematical Practice 1, "Make sense of problems and persevere in solving them."

It is interesting that Jose, the same student who believed the orange would represent the whole, is the one who finds out how to represent both fractional amounts of the same original length whole by combining a red rod and an orange rod. However, the work of the lesson is not complete once Jose determines these representations; the teacher now brings everyone's attention to Jose as he explains. He solidifies his understanding as he has the opportunity to explain his thinking to others. The other students must now make sense of his reasoning. Often, hearing a peer explain a concept is more impactful than hearing a teacher explain it. An underlying message of this lesson is that true understanding of the mathematics can be encouraged through peer-to-peer conversation and discourse. Allowing students to explain and make sense of one another's mathematical understandings provides them with a means to build conceptual understanding.

Once you establish your expectations, rules, norms, and discourse patterns, you must provide students with support throughout small-group instruction.

Supporting Students to Engage in Discourse

Although it is natural for students to engage in conversations, they may find it less comfortable to engage in the types of conversations we've discussed regarding meaningful mathematical discourse. Students may enter the classroom with certain notions about their role in the process of learning mathematics. There are many practices to consider as you challenge these preconceived ideas and support your students to see their roles as active participants in the sense-making process.

In chapter 2 (page 38), you viewed a small-group video in which grade 5 students solved a task involving sharing cookies among five people. In the next video, you will see grade 5 students engaged in an extension task that requires them to add fractions. View the video lesson Add Fractions With Unlike Denominators through the lens of examining teacher moves that support discourse. As you turn your attention to the discourse of the lesson, consider the guiding questions in figure 3.6.

Add Fractions With Unlike Denominators:
SolutionTree.com/GR5AddFractions

- How does the teacher use questioning to elicit student thinking?
- What is the teacher able to determine based on student discourse?
- How does the teacher respond to errors?
- How does the focus on language help students construct meaning of the lesson's mathematical concepts?

Figure 3.6: Guiding questions for observing teacher moves that support discourse in a small-group lesson.

As with the related lesson discussed in chapter 2 (page 38), this small-group task highlights making sense of the mathematics over solving the problem using an equation. The teacher removes the vocabulary terms *numerator* and *denominator* from the conversation. This move purposefully establishes that she expects the students to apply reasoning and understanding to their solution processes. Too often, teachers use and expect students to use vocabulary, like the terms *numerator* and *denominator*, without taking the time to make sure that students have made personal connections to the meaning behind the terms. Students may be able to use the vocabulary but still lack the foundational understanding of what exactly they are discussing. By removing the formal vocabulary, the teacher provides an opportunity for students to make sense of the underlying meaning of the mathematics through the use of everyday language. This, in turn, engages the students in a discussion that will link meaning to the vocabulary words *numerator* and *denominator*. She asks the students what they want to start drawing and then supports the discussion that follows by facilitating the students as they build a shared understanding of what the problem requires, bringing meaning to adding fractions with unlike denominators.

When she states she is "changing the rules" with the task, the teacher provides an opportunity for students to share their thinking about a challenging problem that requires deep understanding. She asks the students to determine the biggest unbroken piece of cookie that could be given to each person. This challenge provokes a couple of responses from the students.

Notice how the teacher does not even hint at whether the students are correct as they make guesses of one-half and three-fourths. Although it would be more efficient for her to tell the students that the biggest unbroken piece possible to give each person is one-half, it would require the trade-off that *she* provides strategies and information. Instead, she places the ownership of developing strategies mainly on the students. The teacher facilitates the process by asking the students whether they are right and encourages them to try the strategies they suggest. The students' explorations are important because they engage the students in making sense of the application of fractions in context.

The role of the teacher is to question and support the students' processes. When the teacher follows this role, the students' engagement in the discussion is evident and conversational. This starkly contrasts with what often occurs when teachers take on the role of providing information to students. As the teacher in this video questions, "How would you . . . ?" "Are we done?" "What are we going to do with it?" and so on, she emphasizes that she expects students to be active participants in the conversation. Her questioning on the size of the piece that is one-twentieth purposefully causes the students to apply other related details they know about recognizing and naming fractional parts of a whole. The teacher anticipates that students will make an error in naming this fractional amount, and rather than correct it, she questions the students to bring their awareness to the importance of identifying the whole in relation to the fractional amount. Students verbalize their newfound understanding, such as when Carter, the student in the gray T-shirt, says, "If this is divided into fifths, every single piece of a fourth would have to be divided into fifths, which would equal a total of twenty pieces." As a result, they begin to solidify the concept. Because the students' skills are still developing, they need additional time to make sense of the task at hand and to make the connection to calling that piece *one-twentieth*.

It is clear that the teacher's strategies effectively focus the students' attention on the expectation that they make sense of the mathematics. It is also clear that students are familiar with the rule, "Own and share your thinking." This is evident when Carter, who originally offered the correct solution of one-twentieth, asks, "Wait, how would it be one-twentieth?" He could have just gone along with what the majority stated, but instead, he feels comfortable sharing his confusion, because this discourse norm has been established during the small-group lesson.

Once the students have identified what each person would receive, they go about naming the amount as a fraction. Remember, the teacher stated that students could not use the terms *numerator* and *denominator*. Notice how this constraint leads students to instead rely on the context of the parts of a cookie. This provides a tangible and meaningful connection as students now make the link between the drawn representation of the cookie and the practicality of adding fractions with unlike denominators. Rather than allowing the students to say that they must find a common denominator, the teacher requires them to maintain the context of the cookie. By doing this, students have an opportunity to relate to their drawings and see the purpose of renaming the pieces of cookie. They are able to use the representation to visualize and describe equivalent fractions.

Once the students have renamed the fractional parts to each represent twentieths, they work to add the fractions. Again, they need a reminder to not use the term *numerator*. By having the students provide their explanation in terms of the cookie, the teacher helps them accomplish more than just applying a procedure to obtain an answer. They make sense of the procedure in a way that is likely to solidify their understanding of what occurs when they ultimately use the terminology and procedures for finding a common denominator and adding the numerators to find the sum of fractions with unlike denominators.

You may find it helpful to have table 3.2 on hand as you engage with and support your students during small-group instruction. We encourage teachers and administrators to transparently state the actions they are consciously working toward improving so they can serve as a support and accountability system for one another.

Table 3.2: Supporting Students Through Actions and Expectations

Teacher Actions to Support Student Discourse	Expectations for Students	Practices to Avoid
The teacher allows students to take the lead in conversations.	Students have a primary role in solving meaningful problems.	The teacher holds sole responsibility for explanations of concepts.
The teacher provides time for students to solve problems.	Students provide solution strategies and explain their thinking.	The teacher leads students to correct answers too quickly.
The teacher responds neutrally to students' responses.	Students seek to understand and state when they disagree.	The teacher provides positive responses, including facial expressions, only to correct answers.
The teacher questions students to facilitate understanding.	Students persevere in the problem-solving process.	The teacher talks more than students.
The teacher approaches incorrect answers with intent to understand and highlight students' thinking.	Students understand that errors are opportunities for sharing and learning.	The teacher ignores incorrect answers and focuses only on correct responses.

Visit go.SolutionTree.com/mathematics for a free reproducible version of this table.

Teachers should combine these strategies for student support with effective teaching practices for facilitating student discourse. We will highlight several such teaching practices in the following section.

Effective Teaching Practices

There are many teaching practices that one could consider *effective*. Effectiveness itself is determined by achieving the desired outcome. When thinking about discourse during mathematics lessons, there are several practices that will help you accomplish the desired outcome of engaging students in meaningful mathematics. We provide four effective teaching practices compiled from research (NCTM, 2014; Smith & Stein, 2011) and our own experiences.

1. Eliciting student thinking

2. Facilitating discussions

3. Maintaining focus on goals

4. Anticipating and responding to challenges

Eliciting Student Thinking

Teachers often miss important opportunities to explore student thinking. Student thinking can and should go much deeper than writing on a worksheet or responding to a teacher's questions. You have much to gain from truly understanding what your students think about mathematical concepts. An effective method for eliciting students' thinking is to engage them in mathematical discourse, as we have discussed throughout this chapter, and to ask meaningful questions, as we talked about in chapter 2 (page 31). You may also elicit student thinking by choosing a meaningful task. This way, students have an engaging challenge to think and talk about. Once you choose a task, you must allow students to take the time to make sense of the task and apply their reasoning. Finally, it is important to let students know that you value what they have to share. You accomplish this with what you say and what you do, as well as with what you don't say and what you don't do.

In addition to encouraging students to think aloud, it's crucial to help them to engage in meaningful discussions. We will discuss the practice of facilitating discussions next.

Facilitating Discussions

When you present a meaningful task, provide time for exploration, and encourage discussion among students, you empower students to engage in mathematics and to see themselves as capable learners and thinkers. Consider the task in figure 3.7. Take a moment to think about how you would solve this problem before you continue reading. What challenges do you anticipate might arise as students work on this task? What questions could you ask to facilitate discussion among students?

> **Task**
>
> Sasha is taking a flight from Orlando, Florida, to Manchester, New Hampshire. The plane is scheduled to take off at 7:15 a.m. and land at 11:45 a.m. How long should it take Sasha to fly from Orlando to Manchester?

Source: Dixon, Nolan, Adams, Tobias, & Barmoha, 2016, p. 150.

Figure 3.7: Focus task for the video lesson Determine Elapsed Time on an Open Time Line.

In the following video, grade 3 students are challenged to use an open time line to solve the task in figure 3.7. You will notice how the teacher engages the students in the small group with each other. She replaces the typical expectation that students speak to the teacher with a new expectation that students converse with other students in the group. When students provide peer support, they solidify their own understanding and, at the same time, define what it means to be a community of learners.

How might the TQE process lesson-planning tool help you prepare to facilitate discussion during this small-group lesson? Use the tool in figure 2.10 (pages 46–47) to help you think about the questions you might ask students. As you watch the following video, consider how the dialogue is different from the traditional IRE discourse pattern we discussed earlier in the chapter (page 52). Think about how the questions you develop compare to those that the teacher uses to facilitate discourse during the actual lesson. Consider the questions in figure 3.8 to guide you as you watch.

   Determine Elapsed Time on an Open Time Line:
SolutionTree.com/GR3ElapsedTime

- How does the teacher facilitate the discussion?
- What are the expectations for the teacher and for the students?
- What teacher moves are most effective for maintaining the discussion among students?

Figure 3.8: Guiding questions for observing a facilitated discussion in a small-group lesson.

This video begins with a word problem that requires the students to use strategies to find the elapsed time for a flight. Notice that the problem itself establishes the need for students to apply a skill as it relates to a situation. The task does not merely give students a chance to learn and practice a skill. Rather, the task will expose their understanding or perhaps a common error regarding how to determine elapsed time in a realistic scenario.

Observe that the teacher does not tell the students how to solve the problem. She also does not dissect the problem for the students. She simply inquires what the problem is asking so that the students have the opportunity to orient themselves to the task. The teacher checks that students understand the task before they begin working. As we discussed in chapter 1 (page 7), when you allow students to struggle with solving a problem because they don't understand what the task is asking, their struggle is not productive. However, you must be careful to not go too far with your explanations so that you maintain the challenge of the task.

Once the students have had some time to work on the problem, the teacher brings the students' attention to the work of their peers. This is important on several levels. First, it allows students to see that there are multiple ways to approach this task. Also, examining the work of others opens the dialogue to discuss solution pathways. If any students were stuck at this point, they could see the different strategies their peers used and get started using those strategies.

It is as important to carefully consider what the teacher does as it is to consider what the teacher avoids. In this example, the teacher asks specific questions to guide students where she wants them to go in terms of their strategies or to build a shared understanding. Purposefully absent are specific directions from the teacher on how to approach or solve the problem. She focuses her facilitation through the use of effective questioning strategies. How do her questions compare to those you thought of before you viewed the lesson? Planning questions in advance of teaching is a useful way of anticipating strategies for facilitating discussion.

As the teacher brings the focus to how the students verbalize their strategies, she establishes the students' role in the discourse and, in turn, their role in the learning process. This sets the expectation that the students should solve the problem and also be able to explain their process and reasoning. The students are expected to listen to their peers, restate what they hear, and understand their reasoning. As the teacher asks questions such as, "Why do you think he added 5 and then added 40?" she is able to highlight a more efficient strategy for the students who are counting by fives. This question has a clear link to her learning goal, and she purposefully uses it to highlight efficient strategies. Did you notice that the teacher does not evaluate the strategies for the students? Rather, she opens the dialogue and points students in the direction she wants them to go through her questioning.

The line of questioning that follows skillfully leads the students with less efficient strategies to make observations about the number of jumps and to consider the effectiveness of an alternative method. You then see Santiago, in the striped shirt, decide to change his strategy based on this information. That is not to say that students will always respond in this way. Readiness is something that cannot be rushed. Had the teacher insisted that the students use the more efficient strategy, they may or may not have been able to mimic it, and they almost certainly would not have internalized it the way they will when given the opportunity to make choices and then evaluate their work compared to the work of others.

At the end of the video lesson, you see the teacher check back in with the students who initially used the inefficient strategy of making jumps of fives. She does not focus only on Solomon, the student in the blue shirt, because he used an efficient method. She intentionally chooses the efficient method to focus the conversation, but she brings each student into the conversation, making sure that the students have established a shared understanding of finding elapsed time on an open time line. This shared understanding is supported by the teacher's explicit efforts to engage students in Mathematical Practice 3, "Construct viable arguments and critique the reasoning of others."

A challenge that arises as the conversation becomes student centered, with the teacher stepping back into the facilitator role, is ensuring that the conversation moves in an appropriate direction toward achieving the learning goal. It is the teacher's job to maintain students' focus on the small-group lesson's learning goal. We will discuss this practice in the following section.

Maintaining Focus on Goals

Something that has likely stood out as you've watched each video in this book is the way the teachers maintain momentum in each lesson. As you consider discourse during small-group instruction, it is important to remember the goal of the lesson. When strategies or conversations begin to move in a direction that does not align with the learning goal, do not be afraid to facilitate or intervene in a way that will guide students back to the focus of the lesson. If other topics emerge, it is preferable to acknowledge student thinking and discuss re-evaluating those thoughts at a later time. However, if these discussion topics support the goal of the lesson, it makes sense to linger. You, as the teacher, will need to make those decisions in real time while teaching. You will best accomplish this when you have made sense of your learning goal and used the TQE process to prepare to support task implementation and discussion before the lesson begins.

In addition to bringing up ideas and strategies that drift off topic, students may provide you with challenges and unexpected questions during small-group work. We will now discuss how to prepare for and respond to these events.

Anticipating and Responding to Challenges

It can be difficult for students to learn the intricacies of engaging in meaningful discussions. You should anticipate challenges so you can effectively address them when they occur. As the culture in your classroom, especially during small-group instruction, begins to shift, you can expect that some students may remain reluctant to join conversations while others may attempt to dominate discussions. There are several strategies you can employ when dealing with these issues.

When students struggle with contributing to the conversation within a small-group lesson, one helpful strategy is to discuss expectations with students in a clear and specific way. For example, you might hold a class or small-group meeting in which you revisit the expectations for the students. Have students engage with the rules for discourse by asking them to act out examples and nonexamples of following the rules. You may try posting a list of expectations on the wall near the small-group table for easy reference during the lesson. Speaking to students on an individual basis when needed can also be beneficial. If some students are frequently quiet within the small-group discussion, ask them whether they would like you to remind them to engage in conversations, such as by asking them to share their strategies. At the same time, if other students tend to dominate a conversation, talk to them about the value and learning that come with inviting their peers into the conversation.

Just as you should not be the sole authority for determining the validity of a response, you should also not be the sole authority in providing feedback for students' adherence to the norms. Furnishing students with the opportunity to reflect on their actions after a small-group lesson will help them self-monitor their behavior and participation in the conversation. You might invite student reflection by asking, "What discourse rule did you follow well during the lesson? Which rule would you like to follow better next time?" It is important for students to reflect on their contributions to the community of learners and acknowledge their role in forming and maintaining that sense of community. Students can often relate to the idea of fairness and respond well when the lesson focuses on providing equal opportunities for everyone to participate.

Conclusion

Student discourse provides an avenue for students to process and deepen their understanding of mathematics. Encouraging students to speak to one another about their thinking is simply the first step in creating a community of learners. Teachers must also be mindful about *how* students contribute to the conversation and ensure *all* students are responsible for contributing to the learning. Paying close attention to discourse patterns and creating and maintaining classroom norms and rules by setting clear expectations will help you keep the focus on the students, and ultimately the learning goal, responding to challenges along the way.

We have explored best practices in small-group instruction, identified how the TQE process will support planning and implementation of effective lessons, and drawn attention to the types of student discourse that will lead to deeper learning of mathematics. In the following epilogue, let's see how these components of small-group instruction come together by observing two lessons and considering next steps for your practice and the practice of those you support.

How to Tie It All Together

You have had the opportunity to explore best practices in small-group instruction, including heterogeneous groups when exploring concepts, planning and implementing instruction using the TQE process, and supporting productive discourse. In this chapter, you will look for these practices as well as others as you watch classroom videos featuring one primary and one intermediate classroom. We will then discuss next steps as you prepare to implement these small-group processes in your classroom and invite you to reflect on the key takeaways from this book.

A Primary-Grade Example

Watch the kindergarten video lesson Define Attributes for Two-Dimensional Shapes, and reflect on your observations related to best practices in small-group instruction before reading further. See figure E.1 for questions to guide your observation.

Define Attributes for Two-Dimensional Shapes:
SolutionTree.com/GRKDefineAttributes

- What best practices for small-group instruction are evident in the lesson?
- What aspects of the TQE process do you see?
- How are students engaged in meaningful discourse?

Figure E.1: Guiding questions for observing small-group instruction.

What do you notice as you watch the video? What is the learning goal? Although the teacher does not supply a specific task, she supports the students in their work with polygons. She wants them to name and describe rectangles, squares, and triangles. How does the teacher use questions to uncover common errors? Before this task, she anticipated that students would incorrectly assume that rectangles must have two long sides and two short sides. Teachers who do not have adequate content knowledge for teaching geometry may unintentionally teach this error to students. It is also something many students come to school believing. The teacher in this video ensures she will elicit this error by planning it into her lesson. She deliberately sequences her questions by first asking students to name and describe a rectangle that is not a square and then asking them to do the same for a square. She asks the students to come up with another name for the square to see whether they know that it is also a rectangle; they do not. She uses the

TQE process to select the task and develop the questions to uncover this very common error. She provides tools she has chosen to clearly elicit and address the common error related to the definition of a rectangle. She supports students to use academic language to describe the shapes and to engage in Mathematical Practice 6, "Attend to precision," as she works to correct the common error.

While most of the discourse occurs between the teacher and the students, the students do much of the talking, and the teacher continually supports them to make sense of each other's responses. When the teacher observes that Natalie, the student in the pink shirt, is not contributing to the conversation, the teacher asks her a specific question to pull her into the conversation. The teacher will want to provide future opportunities for the students to talk to one another, using tasks related to this learning goal. She knows that she will need to provide additional tasks because it is obvious that the students' understanding of this challenging learning goal is tenuous. She can make that determination based on the evidence she collects while students engage in the task and answer questions about the attributes of the shapes.

An Intermediate-Grade Example

In the introduction (page 1), we discussed using small-group instruction for the purpose of enrichment. In the next video, you will see the teacher providing an enrichment activity for students who are ready to take their understanding to the next level. The students previously compared two fractional amounts of candy that two different people ate. You likely watched the video of that grade 4 lesson, Compare Fractions With a Linear Model, when you read chapter 3 (page 57). In the initial lesson, the students decided that Jordan ate more candy by lining up Cuisenaire rods that represented each candy bar. Although they accurately determined who ate more of a candy bar, the students did not determine how much more of his candy bar Jordan ate.

Watch the video of the grade 4 lesson Subtract Fractions With a Linear Model, and reflect on what you've learned about best practices for small-group instruction. Use the following questions in figure E.2 to guide your thinking.

   Subtract Fractions With a Linear Model:
SolutionTree.com/GR4SubtractFractions

- How does the teacher use the small-group structure to meet the learning goal?
- How does the teacher use questioning to elicit student thinking and sense making?
- How does the teacher act as a facilitator during the lesson?

Figure E.2: Guiding questions for observing small-group instruction.

In this video, we see that the teacher does not use the small-group structure to disseminate information to students. Rather, she intentionally chooses a task that will help them conceptualize a problem that requires them to subtract fractions with unlike denominators. If you consider what purpose the small-group structure serves in this case, you see that it provides more individualized instruction during a challenging task. The teacher can easily watch the students approach the problem, use the tool provided, and make adjustments. Through the formative assessment process, she is able to offer support when needed. Students can clearly see one another's work and share their thinking across the table. The Cuisenaire rods are a useful tool for this task because students can use them to create a linear model for each fractional part of two different candy bars. How is unproductive struggle minimized? Perhaps you noticed that Conner, the student in the black T-shirt, has reduced vision. For this reason, the teacher describes the Cuisenaire rods that make up each candy bar. Later during the lesson, she helps redirect Cole, the student in the striped shirt, when he lines up the smaller white rods to the length of ⅝ of a candy bar, rather than a whole candy bar. The teacher asks, "What does our candy bar look like again?" so that he can adjust his model. This facilitation move reinforces the established expectation that students maintain ownership of ideas, rather than look to the teacher to make corrections. The teacher's role is to support the students and provide scaffolding just in time rather than just in case.

We've developed a shared understanding of effective small-group instruction through the use of videos throughout this book. You've also had the opportunity to consider each of the strategies you've learned as you viewed the videos in this chapter. Now we invite you to continue considering how to implement these ideas in your own classroom.

Next Steps

How do you bridge your understanding of the shifts in small-group instruction with the implementation of these shifts? The first step is planning. Throughout this book, we have provided you with a variety of guiding questions and a planning tool (figure 2.10, pages 46–47) for preparing to deliver small-group instruction. This is an opportunity for you to revisit the planning tool and use it in an upcoming unit of study. Because planning time is limited, we suggest selecting three lessons within the unit to plan deeply as a collaborative team. We encourage you to revisit the lesson-planning tool in figure 2.10 to support your planning process for the lessons you select.

When planning for a lesson, first consider the learning goal. Once you have a strong understanding of the learning you want students to achieve, reflect on how you will group students to support their engagement with the learning goal. Some learning goals may be best achieved through whole-group instruction, while others are more suited for small groups. Next, you should consider the task. Remember to think about the cognitive demand of the task. At times, it may be appropriate to use a lower-cognitive-demand task. On the other hand, a higher-cognitive-demand task has the potential to promote students' engagement in higher-level thinking, which may be necessary to achieve the learning goal. Selecting a task that aligns with your learning goal will provide you with further insight regarding the composition of the grouping that will support student learning. If students need to gain conceptual understanding, then you may select a heterogeneous grouping. If the goal focuses on a procedural skill, then you may decide to select a homogeneous group of students.

In addition to choosing a grouping, think about common errors that might surface during the lesson. The mathematical tools you provide may serve as a platform for addressing these errors as well as building students' mathematical understandings. Now that you have an idea of the learning goal, the task, common errors related to the learning goal, and tools you will provide, you should determine which Mathematical Practices to target throughout the lesson. This will help when developing questions that advance student understanding. Questions should also focus on addressing anticipated common errors, providing scaffolding, and gathering evidence. Collecting evidence of student learning within a formative assessment process plays a large role in shifting your instruction to meet the needs of your students. Plan for the type of evidence you will collect throughout the task, and consider how the evidence will affect the line of questioning you implement.

Once you have a well-developed plan and you have implemented the lesson, reflect on how the decisions you made and the instructional strategies you used affected student learning outcomes. Record the unanticipated errors that arose, and consider how you might address these in future teaching of the topic.

Invitation for Reflection

In the introduction (page 1), we invited you to deeply reflect on your current beliefs and practices regarding small-group instruction. We encouraged you to read this book together as teachers and administrators and reflect on how this book challenges your beliefs and practices. Participating in this type of reflection on your current practices is necessary before change can occur. Think back on the instructional philosophies and practices presented in this book. What challenged your thinking? What changes will you make in your instruction based on these new thoughts? What support do you need as you consider making changes?

According to University of Kentucky educational psychology professor Thomas R. Guskey (2017), changes in teachers' beliefs and attitudes occur only *after* teachers have changed their classroom practice and seen positive results in student learning. This means that you might not be compelled to change your mindset on small-group instruction until you implement these practices with your students. Challenge yourself to implement your learning from the videos and discussions presented in this book. Take note of the differences you see in student thinking and reasoning about mathematics as a result of the strategies you implement. How will you use your knowledge of effective small-group instruction in mathematics to support students in making sense of mathematics? Learning these strategies is a process. We hope you allow yourself the time for your own important productive struggle. Use the resources available to you and your collaborative team—but most of all, enjoy the journey!

APPENDIX A

Sample Lesson Plan for Grades K–2 Using TQE Process Lesson-Planning Tool

Figure A.1 is a sample lesson plan for the task in figure 1.2 (page 8). The lesson plan was created using Dixon et al.'s (2016) TQE process lesson-planning tool.

TQE Process Lesson-Planning Tool
Learning Goal
Students will connect the concept of adding three-digit numbers with regrouping to a standard algorithm.
What are your considerations for grouping students? Is it appropriate to use small-group instruction to meet this learning goal?
Students struggle with understanding the "why" behind the traditional algorithm for addition. In this lesson, students will be asked to link the concept of regrouping using base ten blocks to the traditional algorithm. Moderately heterogeneous grouping sets up an environment for mathematical discourse, in which students will be encouraged to use place value language to explain the algorithm to one another. Students who can follow the steps of the traditional algorithm may struggle to understand the connection to the base ten blocks. Students who struggle with the steps of the algorithm may be able to explain the connection. The small-group setting allows growth opportunities for both sets of students. The small-group setting will also provide an avenue for holding each student accountable for participating in the conversation as they develop conceptual understanding.

Task	**Record your task here:**
This high-cognitive-demand task links to the learning goal and allows students to engage in Mathematical Practices.	*The candy shop at Sweet Tooth Elementary School has 376 candies. If the school orders another 258 candies, how many will the store have then?*

What common errors might be elicited as students work on this task?
The problem is designed to see if students can connect place value concepts to the traditional algorithm for addition. Students may correctly group ten ones but then incorrectly exchange. They may also miscount the numbers as they regroup a set of ten to the next place value. When regrouping fourteen ones into a set of ten and four ones, students may call the set of ten a "one" instead of a ten. This same incorrect understanding might be applied when regrouping the tens into a group of one hundred.
What tools will you use to support students to engage with the task?
Students will be provided with base ten blocks and a whiteboard and marker to solve the problem. Making both concrete manipulatives and a way for students to solve the problem with a representation or using numbers in an abstract way available will allow for a connection to be made between the concept of regrouping and the traditional algorithm for addition. This will also provide an opportunity to gather evidence in regard to the tools chosen by each student and how they interact with the tools.

What Mathematical Practices do you anticipate the students engaging in as they work on this task?

Mathematical Practice 6: Attend to precision.

Mathematical Practice 7: Look for and make use of structure.

Questions	Record your questions here:
These questions facilitate students to engage in the Mathematical Practices, elicit common errors and evidence of conceptual understanding, and offer scaffolding just in time.	*Is that a "one"? What does it mean in your problem?* *What does that "one" represent?* *What does your classmate mean by that?* *If I use the base ten blocks to add the ones together, what do I record here?* *How you can show the addition with the base ten blocks?* *Then what happened? What did you do with that "fourteen"?* *How many ones did you regroup to make a ten?* *Where do you have this one ten recorded?* *How could you relate the use of the base ten blocks to the algorithm?*
Evidence	**Record examples of evidence you will collect here:**
This evidence is used to determine whether students have met the learning goal and to uncover common errors.	*Student regrouping using the base ten blocks* *Students' use of place value language while describing the traditional algorithm* *Student calculation using the traditional algorithm* *Student responses and justifications to teacher questions*

Figure A.1: Sample lesson plan for the multidigit addition task.

APPENDIX B

Sample Lesson Plan for Grades 3–5 Using TQE Process Lesson-Planning Tool

Figure B.1 is a sample lesson plan for the task in the video on page 59. The lesson plan was created using Dixon et al.'s (2016) TQE process lesson-planning tool.

TQE Process Lesson-Planning Tool	
Learning Goal *Students will make sense of adding fractions with unlike denominators.*	
What are your considerations for grouping students? Is it appropriate to use small-group instruction to meet this learning goal? *Since the purpose of the lesson is for students to develop conceptual understanding of adding fractions with unlike denominators, moderately heterogeneous grouping will enable students to learn from one another's thinking. Small-group instruction will allow the teacher to collect evidence regarding each student's understanding and ask individualized questions to build upon students' current knowledge of fraction concepts.*	
Task This high-cognitive-demand task links to the learning goal and allows students to engage in Mathematical Practices.	**Record your task here:** *Brandon shared four cookies equally between himself and his four friends. How much of a cookie should each person get if each person is given the largest, same-size unbroken piece of cookie to start before Brandon fairly shares the rest of the cookies?*
What common errors might be elicited as students work on this task? *Students might struggle with naming the fractions. They might mistake $\frac{1}{4}$ for $\frac{1}{3}$, as the circle will be split into a total of three pieces, without realizing that the pieces are of unequal size. They may make the same mistake when naming $\frac{1}{20}$ and call each piece $\frac{1}{8}$. They might also confuse the whole as they name fractions. The problem is designed to see if they name the $\frac{1}{20}$ size piece as $\frac{1}{5}$ because it is $\frac{1}{5}$ of $\frac{1}{4}$.*	
What tools will you use to support students to engage with the task? *Students will be provided with a whiteboard and marker for representing the problem. A whiteboard will allow for flexible thinking and reasoning when splitting each cookie. Fraction manipulatives will not be provided as this could limit the number of ways students might choose to split each cookie.*	
What Mathematical Practices do you anticipate the students engaging in as they work on this task? *Mathematical Practice 1: Make sense of problems and persevere in solving them.* *Mathematical Practice 7: Look for and make use of structure.*	

Questions	Record your questions here:
These questions facilitate students to engage in the Mathematical Practices, elicit common errors and evidence of conceptual understanding, and offer scaffolding just in time.	*What would person A get altogether?* *What would you name that piece?* *How does that align with our rule that each person must get the biggest unbroken piece of cookie first?* *What else might you try?* *Is person E getting the same amount as person A? How do you know?* *Do you agree?* *How did you get ¼?* *Why do you think it is ⅓? Why is it ⅛?* *What kind of pieces do they need to be?* *Where do you get ½₀ from?*
Evidence	**Record examples of evidence you will collect here:**
This evidence is used to determine whether students have met the learning goal and to uncover common errors.	*Student drawings* *How students name each piece of cookie* *Student responses and justifications to teacher questions*

Figure B.1: Sample lesson plan for Adding Fractions With Unlike Denominators task.

References and Resources

Brooks, L. A. (2014). *Replacing the "raise your hand to speak" rule with new social and sociomathematical norms in an elementary mathematics classroom* (Doctoral dissertation). University of Central Florida, Orlando.

Brooks, L. A., & Dixon, J. K. (2013). Changing the rules to increase discourse. *Teaching Children Mathematics, 20*(2), 84–89.

Butler, F. M., Miller, S. P., Crehan, K., Babbitt, B., & Pierce, T. (2003). Fraction instruction for students with mathematics disabilities: Comparing two teaching sequences. *Learning Disabilities: Research and Practice, 18*(2), 99–111.

Carpenter, T. P., Fennema, E., Franke, M. L., Levi, L., & Empson, S. B. (2015). *Children's mathematics: Cognitively guided instruction* (2nd ed.). Portsmouth, NH: Heinemann.

Dean, C. B., Hubbell, E. R., Pitler, H., & Stone, B. (2012). *Classroom instruction that works: Research-based strategies for increasing student achievement* (2nd ed.). Alexandria, VA: Association for Supervision and Curriculum Development.

Dixon, J. K., Adams, T. L., & Nolan, E. C. (2015). *Beyond the Common Core: A handbook for mathematics in a PLC at Work, grades K–5*. T. D. Kanold (Ed.). Bloomington, IN: Solution Tree Press.

Dixon, J. K., Andreasen, J. B., & Stephan, M. (2009). Establishing social and sociomathematical norms in an undergraduate mathematics content course for prospective teachers: The role of the instructor. In D. S. Mewborn & H. S. Lee (Eds.), *Scholarly practices and inquiry in the preparation of mathematics teachers* (Vol. 6, pp. 43–66). San Diego, CA: Association of Mathematics Teacher Educators.

Dixon, J. K., Nolan, E. C., & Adams, T. L. (2016). *What does it mean to teach mathematics with focus, coherence, and rigor, and how is it achieved?* Bloomington, IN: Solution Tree.

Dixon, J. K., Nolan, E. C., Adams, T. L., Brooks, L. A., & Howse, T. D. (2016). *Making sense of mathematics for teaching grades K–2*. Bloomington, IN: Solution Tree Press.

Dixon, J. K., Nolan, E. C., Adams, T. L., Tobias, J. M., & Barmoha, G. (2016). *Making sense of mathematics for teaching grades 3–5*. Bloomington, IN: Solution Tree Press.

Fisher, D., & Frey, N. (2014). *Better learning through structured teaching: A framework for the gradual release of responsibility* (2nd ed.). Alexandria, VA: Association for Supervision and Curriculum Development.

Fuchs, L. S., Fuchs, D., & Compton, D. L. (2012). The early prevention of mathematics difficulty: Its power and limitations. *Journal of Learning Disabilities, 45*(3), 257–269.

Gresham, G., & Little, M. (2012). RtI in math class. *Teaching Children Mathematics, 19*(1), 20–29.

Guskey, T. R. (1985). Staff development and teacher change. *Educational Leadership, 42*(7), 57–60.

Guskey, T. R. (2017). Where do you want to get to? *Learning Professional, 36*(2), 32–37.

Huinker, D., & Bill, V. (2017). *Taking action: Implementing effective mathematics teaching practices in K–grade 5.* M. S. Smith (Ed.). Reston, VA: National Council of Teachers of Mathematics.

McGatha, M. B., & Bay-Williams, J. M. (2013). Making shifts toward proficiency. *Teaching Children Mathematics, 20*(3), 162–170.

Mehan, H. (1979). *Learning lessons: Social organization in the classroom.* Cambridge, MA: Harvard University Press.

Nathan, M. J., Eilam, B., & Kim, S. (2007). To disagree, we must also agree: How intersubjectivity structures and perpetuates discourse in a mathematics classroom. *Journal of the Learning Sciences, 16*(4), 523–563.

National Council of Teachers of Mathematics. (1991). *Professional standards for teaching mathematics.* Reston, VA: Author.

National Council of Teachers of Mathematics. (2014). *Principles to actions: Ensuring mathematical success for all.* Reston, VA: Author.

National Governors Association Center for Best Practices & Council of Chief State School Officers. (2010). *Common Core State Standards for mathematics.* Washington, DC: Authors. Accessed at www.corestandards.org/assets/CCSSI_Math%20Standards.pdf on January 4, 2018.

Smith, M. S., & Stein, M. K. (2011). *5 practices for orchestrating productive mathematics discussions.* Reston, VA: National Council of Teachers of Mathematics.

Smith, M. S., & Stein, M. K. (2012). Selecting and creating mathematical tasks: From research to practice. In G. Lappan, M. S. Smith, & E. Jones (Eds.), *Rich and engaging mathematical tasks: Grades 5–9* (pp. 4–10). Reston, VA: National Council of Teachers of Mathematics.

Stein, M. K., Engle, R. A., Smith, M. S., & Hughes, E. K. (2008). Orchestrating productive mathematical discussions: Five practices for helping teachers move beyond show and tell. *Mathematical Thinking and Learning, 10*(4), 313–340.

Stein, M. K., & Smith, M. S. (1998). Mathematical tasks as a framework for reflection: From research to practice. *Mathematics Teaching in the Middle School, 3*(4), 268–275.

Vygotsky, L. (1994). The development of academic concepts in school aged children. In R. van der Veer & J. Valsiner (Eds.), *The Vygotsky reader* (pp. 355–370). Oxford, England: Blackwell. (Original work published 1934)

Walshaw, M., & Anthony, G. (2008). The teacher's role in classroom discourse: A review of recent research into mathematics classrooms. *Review of Educational Research, 78*(3), 516–551.

Wiliam, D. (2018). *Embedded formative assessment* (2nd ed.). Bloomington, IN: Solution Tree Press.

Yackel, E., & Cobb, P. (1996). Sociomathematical norms, argumentation, and autonomy in mathematics. *Journal for Research in Mathematics Education, 27*(4), 458–477.

Index

students' roles in, 22–23
teacher's role in, 10–22
use of term, 1
Smith, M. S., 35
solution processes, 36
Standards for Mathematical Practice, 3
See also under Mathematical Practice
Stein, M. K., 35
student engagement, supporting, 59–62
student responses
anticipating, 35
mathematical connections between, 35
monitoring, 35
selecting students and, 35
sequencing, 35
students' roles
in discourse, 51
in small-group instruction, 22–23
student thinking, eliciting, 62

T

Taking Action: Implementing Effective Mathematics Teaching Practices in K–Grade 5 (Huinker and Bill), 13–14
task icon, 6
tasks, 34–39
teacher's role
in discourse, 51
in small-group instruction, 10–22
Tobias, J. M., 4
tools, 26–28
TQE (tasks, questions, and evidence) process, 5
evidence, 42–45
lesson-planning tool, 45, 46–47, 71–74
questions, 40–42
role of, 31–34
tasks, 34–39

U

unproductive struggle, 19

V

videos, list of
Add Fractions With Unlike Denominators, 59–61
Add Three-Digit Numbers With Regrouping, 8–10, 14, 15, 27
Compare Fractions With a Linear Model, 57–59, 68
Compare Objects Using Indirect Measurement, 24–25, 27
Count and Compare Cubes, 49–51
Define Attributes for Two-Dimensional Shapes, 67–68
Determine Elapsed Time on an Open Time Line, 62–64
Find Area and Order by Size, 56
Locate and Name Decimals on a Number Line to the Hundredths Place, 32–34, 35–36
Locate and Name Decimals on a Number Line to the Thousandths Place, 40–42
Make Sense of the Long Division Algorithm, 17–18, 26
Name Fractions With Unlike Denominators, 38–39
Relate Number of Partitioned Pieces to Size of Pieces, 43–45
Order and Compute With Coins, 20–21
Subtract Fractions With a Linear Model, 68–69
Vygotsky, L., 51

W

Walshaw, M., 40
Wiliam, D., 16, 42

Y

Yackel, E., 23

Making Sense of Mathematics for Teaching Grades K–2
Juli K. Dixon, Edward C. Nolan, Thomasenia Lott Adams, Lisa A. Brooks, and Tashana D. Howse

Develop a deep understanding of mathematics. With this user-friendly resource, grades K–2 teachers will explore strategies and techniques to effectively learn and teach significant mathematics concepts and provide all students with the precise, accurate information they need to achieve academic success.
BKF695

Making Sense of Mathematics for Teaching Grades 3–5
Juli K. Dixon, Edward C. Nolan, Thomasenia Lott Adams, Jennifer M. Tobias, and Guy Barmoha

Develop a deep understanding of mathematics. With this user-friendly resource, grades 3–5 teachers will explore strategies and techniques to effectively learn and teach significant mathematics concepts and provide all students with the precise, accurate information they need to achieve academic success.
BKF696

Making Sense of Mathematics for Teaching Grades K–2
[DVD/Facilitator's Guide/Paperback]
Juli K. Dixon, Edward C. Nolan, Thomasenia Lott Adams, Lisa A. Brooks, and Tashana D. Howse

This video program will help educators develop a deeper understanding of mathematics and more effectively provide mathematics instruction in grades K–2. Included is the companion paperback book, *Making Sense of Mathematics for Teaching Grades K–2*.
DVF067

Making Sense of Mathematics for Teaching Grades 3–5
[DVD/Facilitator's Guide/Paperback]
Juli K. Dixon, Edward C. Nolan, Thomasenia Lott Adams, Jennifer M. Tobias, and Guy Barmoha

This multifaceted workshop utilizes video, discussion, and activities to help teachers engage in mathematics as both learners and instructors. It also serves to provide a shared vision of classrooms where teachers and students are engaged in meaningful mathematics learning experiences.
DVF068

Making Sense of Mathematics for Teaching series
Juli K. Dixon, Edward C. Nolan, Thomasenia Lott Adams, Janet B. Andreasen, Guy Barmoha, Lisa A. Brooks, Erhan Selcuk Haciomeroglu, Tashana D. Howse, George J. Roy, Farshid Safi, and Jennifer M. Tobias

This user-friendly series presents an authentic look inside real mathematics classrooms, inviting teachers to become learners. Explore strategies and techniques to effectively learn and teach significant mathematics concepts, and provide every student with the experiences needed to achieve academic success in mathematics.
BKF695, BKF696, BKF697, BKF698

Solution Tree | Press
a division of
Solution Tree

Visit SolutionTree.com or call 800.733.6786 to order.

Wait! Your professional development journey doesn't have to end with the last pages of this book.

We realize improving student learning doesn't happen overnight. And your school or district shouldn't be left to puzzle out all the details of this process alone.

No matter where you are on the journey, we're committed to helping you get to the next stage.

Take advantage of everything from **custom workshops** to **keynote presentations** and **interactive web and video conferencing**. We can even help you develop an action plan tailored to fit your specific needs.

Let's get the conversation started.

Call 888.763.9045 today.

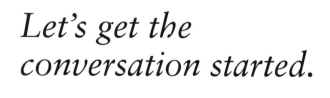

 SolutionTree.com